P9-DIH-255

Healing Ministries

Conversations on the Spiritual Dimensions of Health Care

by

Joseph H. Fichter

PAULIST PRESS
New York/Mahwah

Book design by Celine M. Allen

Copyright © 1986 by
Joseph H. Fichter

All rights reserved. No part of this book may be reproduced or transmitted
in any form or by any means, electronic or mechanical, including photo-
copying, recording or by any information storage and retrieval system
without permission in writing from the Publisher.

Library of Congress Cataloging-in-Publication Data

Fichter, Joseph Henry, 1908–
    Healing ministries.

    1. Health—Religious aspects—Christianity.
2. Medicine—Religious aspects—Christianity.
3. Medical personnel—interviews. I. Title.
BT732.F53   1986   261.8'321   86-91547
ISBN 0-8091-2807-1 (pbk.)

Published by Paulist Press
997 Macarthur Boulevard
Mahwah, New Jersey 07430

Printed and bound in the
United States of America

CONTENTS

Lincoln Christian College

PREFACE

Testimony of Health Care Experts

The central question in these interviews focuses on the health care professional's personal responsibility for the spiritual dimension of the healing process. How do the daily practitioners of the art of healing, curing and caring bring God into the sick room? How do they understand, and deliver, the so-called "benefits of religion" in their direct contact with the ailing patients who come to them for help?

The responses of these twenty health professionals are based on their experience and training and are expressed from the perspective of their specialized roles. These highly qualified individuals were selected from more than a hundred persons I interviewed in the course of research for my study of *Religion and Pain*. They reveal their special interest in the sick patients, the particular concern and emphasis they bring to that relationship, and their specific professional perspective. Only one generalization fits them all: the holistic concept of healing. They are convinced that the high technology of medicine is not fully adequate to deal with sickness and suffering unless it includes one's relationship of dependence upon a loving and compassionate God.

Nowadays the setting for the spiritual encounter between the person who is sick and the person who ministers to the sick is the modern hospital, staffed by varieties of health care professionals. There are exceptions. Psychiatrists often deal with individuals in the privacy of their office. Some physicians also keep office hours, but they are less and less likely to make "house calls," and they prefer to assign their patients to a hospital room. The hospice movement is gradually substituting home care for hospital care, and is attracting unpaid volunteers more often than well-paid professionals. The Christian practice of visiting the sick at home is increasingly performed by lay people, eucharistic ministers, who bring the sacrament to shut-ins.

Since there is a concentration of health care in the hospital setting it is to be expected that people trained in clinical pastoral ministry are the most numerous interviewees. Among the nine hospital chaplains who speak for themselves, two are religious sisters and one an ordained Lutheran woman pastor. The eleven other professional roles here represented include four psychiatrists (of whom two are women), four nurses, two surgeons, and one social worker. They are evenly divided by gender: ten women and ten men. From the criterion of ordination, most are lay persons, of whom two are Episcopalian and one Jewish. Among the eight ordained clergy persons, one is Lutheran, one Presbyterian, and six Roman Catholic.

Eight of our interviewees are employed in church-related hospitals where the spiritual care of the sick is built into the whole institutional philosophy and practice. Here one finds nurses and doctors, sisters, ministers, and administrators who are personally dedicated and institutionally supported in the spiritual dimensions of health care. The other hospitals, public and proprietary, demonstrate varying degrees of appreciation for the support of clinical pastoral ministry. Some are reluctant to write into their budget the financial cost of a formal department of well-trained pastoral care professionals. There are still some hospital administrators—a decreasing number—who want the local denominations and dioceses to provide a health care ministry at the church's expense.

Before turning on the tape recorder for each of these interviews I promised a kind of rough anonymity which would prevent specific identification of the participants. All of them said, however, that they were willing to speak "for the record," but I felt they would be more comfortable in print if I omitted family names and provided pseudonymous first names. I am, of course, grateful for their willingness to tell their stories and to cooperate in this opportunity to provide both realistic experience and thoughtful reflection on that experience. I am thankful also to Helen Jones who should not be wrapped in anonymity for the research skills and communication expertise she contributed to the production of this book.

I

Imagination and Well-Being

Dr. Edward, a devout Episcopalian
physician, teaches clinical hypnosis at
a large university medical school

Is religion part of your academic lectures in hypnotherapy?

Only in an indirect way. This is an elective course for
credit in the medical school, and you probably know that
hypnosis was forbidden in medical practice from the time of
Mesmer until 1968, but we now have about four thousand
doctors involved in it. The procedure is really largely dealing
with the imagination. You can imagine that you are ill and
you can imagine that you are well, and I do devote some time
to the significance of religion. The thrust of my lecture is not
what religion is doing to the patient, but what the patient is
doing to religion, and what I think my students need to understand, as adults, about religion other than what they were
taught as children. You teach a child what a child can understand, but many medical students learned nothing about religion since they were children. As physicians they may miss
a lot of things where they can help patients if they don't know
anything about religion.

One of the common emotional problems, mainly with
gastrointestinal disorders, chronic diarrhea and this type of

ailment, is anger and resentment. When I get into hypnoan-
alysis of this, and get the patient to go back to when it started,
frequently it will reach some episode in childhood where the
child perceived an injustice with the father or mother, and the
real anger about being unfairly treated, and this resentment
just stays there. The treatment for resentment and anger has
been around for two thousand years, and this is scriptural
and spiritual. The parent is not suffering; it is the patient who
has the ulcer and it has been going on long enough, so then
I say: "Why don't you forgive him?" People usually don't
think about forgiving someone who doesn't ask to be forgiven. You forgive somebody, or at least you think about it,
when the person asks to be forgiven. So, what I do in the therapeutic situation is to become the advocate of the parent, or
whoever it was, and I ask them to forgive the injustice. Sometimes the patient says: "I don't see that. I just cannot do it."
And the pain remains.

*That's chronic pain. Do you ever say: "You've got to learn to live
with it"?*

I think that's a terrible thing to say to anybody, because
if you take it literally it means that the only way to get rid of
pain is to die, and the subconscious mind does take it that
way. So you've locked the patient into the acceptance as a
valid fact that he is going to die unless he learns to live with
pain. I think physicians who say that to people are frustrated
and don't want to tell the truth, which is: "I don't know what
to do for you. I don't know what's the matter with you." And
that's humiliating because it's an admission that if we don't
know what the diagnosis is we don't know what the prognosis is. Instead we say: "You've got to learn to live with it,"
which may not be true at all because many types of chronic
pain do remit.

I think there is always a reason when somebody hurts. It
may not be emotional in every case; it may be a matter of sur-
vival. I have a series of patients who are in constant pain. In
some cases, even with the pain of cancer, you can at times
sleep comfortably. But there are patients who say, "The pain

is there all the time. It may be sharper or less, but I am never without it. If I go to sleep I know it is there because when I wake up it is the first thing I notice." Put these patients in hypnosis and you can revivify some part of their past as though they were there again. When we go back to when the pain started we find that three things occur simultaneously. First is some kind of mental disorientation; it may have been a concussion or a stroke. It is a very frightening thing to be disoriented. Second, in that condition they perceive them-selves as being terribly in danger of death; and third, the pain is there and it may be in the head or in the chest; and in the intensive care ward they may be over-sedated. They are afraid they are going to die because of whatever happened to them. The only way they know they are alive is because of that pain, and at an instinctive, subconscious level it is very reassuring. "As long as I've got the pain, I'm still alive." If you subconsciously equate that pain with life, you can't be without it for five minutes. You can let it increase or decrease, but it always has to be there.

How does religion come into that situation?

Probably it doesn't, at least not directly, unless your re-ligion convinces you that there is great value to life even in the midst of pain. What I really have to deal with is breaking the equation that pain equals life. Most people probably are alive and well, which means they are without pain; they are walking; they are talking. What I often find going on in chronic pain patients is the emotion of fear or anger, both of which mobilize hormones in the body that are ultimately harmful. Both fear and anger are ruled out by the lessons of the scripture. I think the epistle to Timothy tells us that the spirit of fear does not come from God, who gives us the spirit of power and love. There is some evidence that people who have religion as a resource often get very good relief from pain and sickness. I've never been to Lourdes, but I've been to the shrine of Saint Anne de Beaupre, and I can only guess that the people who were cured were able to allay their fears by trust in God's power. You see all those crutches there and you have to face the fact that some people walked away.

There are all sorts of disorders in the area of psychosomatic illnesses in which religion may be of real help. This has been demonstrated particularly with kids who are strung out on drugs—LSD, marijuana and even cocaine. I can't put my finger on the statistics but I've read that the kids who are able to "pitch out" tend to be the ones who have a firm religious background. The ones who are lost and who are goners for good are the ones who had no religion to fall back on. You know better than I do in your study of alcoholic clergy that the higher power on whom recovering alcoholics depend is not some voodoo magic. A lot of doctors are frustrated with the fact that their conventional medical practice does not bring much relief to the chronic alcoholic while the spiritual formula of Alcoholics Anonymous has had remarkable success.

Do your patients think their sickness is God's punishment?

Oh yes, very much so, especially with some of the fundamentalists who have a concept of a harsh and judgmental God; and I turn this around by telling them that they are violating the first commandment. They are putting themselves in the place of God; they are usurping a power that only God has to make judgments about who is guilty and who is innocent. If they are true believers they are not entitled to judge themselves.

This is not as simple as it sounds because a person may very well be guilty of some dreadful past sins. Nobody feels guilty who does not have an ethic that recognizes the difference between virtue and vice, good and evil. The problem is not that the sick person may be actually guilty; the problem is in self-punishment. Justice is getting what you deserve, reward if you deserve reward, punishment if you deserve punishment. I can't mete out justice unless I know all the facts, and probably here on earth you will never face a judge who knows all the facts; but in the one place where all the facts are known I'm not asking for justice. I don't want what I deserve; I want mercy.

As a physician I am not going to tell even a guilty person to confess his sins, but I do want him to stop punishing himself. Nevertheless, any person brought up in the Judaeo-Christian tradition knows what that belief promises. If we will repent and turn the judgment over to God where it belongs, he will make the judgment. We don't have that jurisdiction; and we must not act like a God of vengeance instead of a God of forgiveness. I have no hesitation as a doctor to try to dissuade a patient who is misusing his religion and saying, "I have been bad; I am guilty and I deserve this pain." This is not the nature of the Christian religion which is the abundant life with forgiveness and love. If he is going to use scripture as his basis, I may have to come back with a better scripture. At least, for his health's sake, I can get him to appreciate the religious resources he has and say, "Remember what you have been taught is that God loves you and forgives you." I guess what I am saying is that there is no such thing as an unforgivable sin, except defying God, and that is forgivable if you come back to him.

Do you ever pray with your patients?

I wouldn't hesitate to, if a patient asks me to. But if you are going to have a prayer I think that emotionally it means more to have a minister of your own religion lead you in it. It's like calling in the expert. If you are going to have an operation you want the best surgeon. In other words, if I am dealing with someone who wants and needs religious ministry, I don't hesitate to suggest: "Why don't we call your chaplain to see you and help you with this?"

I think we have to recognize different areas of expertise, and what they do may depend on the personalities of different physicians. I want my patients to have everything that is likely to help them get well. It's the same way I recommend a specialist, like a neurologist, to come in and see the patient. It adds to the specialist's credibility if I encourage the patient to follow my recommendation. I think sometimes the patients are intimidated a little bit as though they are afraid the doctor will denigrate the religious administrations. The patient may feel that he wants a priest, but he's afraid the doctor may think that the priest is interfering with the case. I can't do the priest's job. Suppose I suggest extreme unction. Some patients may take this as indicating that they are condemned to die, that they will be receiving the death rite. It is much better if I just recommend the religious expert and leave it to him.

If I know a person is a church-goer but is reluctant to call in his minister or priest I sometimes ask him if he has written a will. If the answer is "yes" as it usually is with the type of patient I have, I will tell him, "You wrote that will long before you needed it because you wanted to have your affairs in good order all the time; and I think it is good for you to be anointed, to get the sacrament of the sick, because you ought to have your spiritual affairs in good order all the time." This just makes it something like a routine act rather than exceptional at the point of death.

This is not unusual for me. I am Episcopalian and I practice my religion, and I believe in it. I don't think that makes me particularly different from other physicians. I do think it makes a difference in health care whether or not a doctor is a religious person. Of course, we all have various and other experiences. I was brought up to be a pretty obsessive-compulsive type. I got sick enough so that I underwent six years of analysis. In that process I got over a couple of fairly serious psychosomatic disorders. I think I quit hating myself and started loving myself, and I have found it a lot easier to love other people.

Do people in a crisis of suffering turn to God?

Not as their first reaction. That hasn't been my experience at all. Turning to God, for religious people, seems to be a secondary phenomenon, when they are moving toward recovery. I treat a lot of trauma injuries, usually resulting from accidents of various kinds. The initial reaction is the first law of nature, self-preservation. This is what's going on with that concussion, and the fear of pain and death. "Am I going to get out of this alive?" That's the primary concern. It is only later, when they are in the hospital and have been examined and reassured, that things are calming down. Then the patient no longer feels: "I've got to preserve myself." Somebody else is there, the doctor, the nurses, to do it for him.

The fear has been removed because the health care people are doing their thing with the patient, but I think what is most important for the patient is not what they are doing for him but the fact that he feels confident to be in their hands. His trust in them takes away his fear, or at least it lessens the fear and, I am convinced, also lessens the pain. Now if you translate that situation to the relationship that a true believer has with God, you find that his trust and confidence in God comes in as the secondary phenomenon I mentioned. It may be a kind of second thought, a double take as they say, in the expression of gratitude for divine health care. Even non-believers almost instinctively are apt to say, "Thank God."

There's another point I want to make, especially about the hospitalized patient. It is that many people don't realize that loneliness is a severe disease. People come to physicians because they hurt and are therefore afraid of what might be wrong with them, but also because they are lonely. Physically, they are not alone. They may have all kinds of relatives and friends, but they feel that nobody cares about them. It doesn't matter to anyone whether they are sick or well, living or dying.

This is an added sickness, particularly for patients who know they are terminally ill. Most people don't mind dying. You don't expect to live forever, but you do mind dying if nobody cares. That's one of the things I learned early with cancer patients. I give them my card with my office number, my exchange number, and my home number. I tell them, "Whenever you need me, I'll come. Call me at any time of day or night, weekends or Christmas." And you do get two phone calls. Within ten days they try it once to test you out. That satisfies them, and the next call is when they really need you. In the meantime, they've got the feeling that somebody does care and can be relied on. I think that's a form of agape.

How do you deal with patients who are completely indifferent to religion?

I want to make clear that a physician is not expected to be an evangelist. You were told by one of my colleagues that I see some value in religion for the benefit of sick people, but all my patients come to me because I am a medical doctor, not because I go to church on Sunday. So, to answer your question, I use my medical knowledge and skills in treating both believers and non-believers. Some patients, and their families, know me well and they know my own beliefs and attitudes. But I don't think that people like to get lectured on religion by their doctor, unless they are already receptive.

From the opposite perspective I think this is the reason why a lot of people won't go to a Freudian psychologist. They have a popular notion of Freudianism which is anti-religious and pro-sex. They want to get their headaches cured but they don't want to hear somebody downgrade their religion. They expect a Freudian psychiatrist to do that. Any number of patients who come to me realize that they are in some kind of a psychological foul-up, but they are not willing to go to a psychiatrist. I think they feel as though they were going to be urged into sexual affairs or other irreligious things, and they say, "I just want to get my headaches cured, not my religion changed."

Religious people who fear Freudianism sometimes also fear hypnotism, and they have to be reassured what hypnotherapy can do and cannot do. Ordinary medical practice tries to relieve pain; hypnotherapy tries to relieve suffering, and it's important to know the difference. Pain is the objective, measurable, neurophysical signal; but suffering is the subjective, emotional, evaluative response. Pain is not as amenable to hypnotherapy, though it is sometimes relieved. When suffering is removed, it appears that pure pain doesn't really hurt so much.

I ought to say that these ideas are shared by the members of the American Society of Clinical Hypnosis, who are dentists, psychologists, surgeons and physicians in all the medical specialties. We have a permanent Committee on

Hypnosis and Religion, of which I am a member. At the annual meeting of the society this committee sponsors one afternoon's program when we give papers and talk about cases and techniques. I gave a paper at the last meeting on the very topic we are talking about, and I don't recall negative criticism from any agnostic members of the society.

Would you care to say whether your medical school is graduating any physicians who are like you?

I'm not sure that would be an improvement over past graduating classes. In my fairly limited contact with the medical students I get the impression that they are concentrating as seriously as we did on the areas of medicine that will get them through the course. There have always been some student groups that talk about moral and ethical aspects of the medical profession. Just last month I talked to about fifty students at a luncheon of the Catholic Campus Club. I tried to describe the kinds of emotional problems, or personality quirks, they will meet in patients, but there was no mention of religion, or of the spiritual aspect of health care.

The more inquisitive medical students ask about the reputation and experiences of Norman Cousins and his insistence that the healing process depends largely on psychological, moral and spiritual factors. He is, of course, in the tradition of physicians like William Osler and Jerome Frank who argued, as I do, that treatment of an illness that does not also minister to the human spirit is "grossly deficient." Medical students may have some confidence in such a statement coming from a member of the medical profession, but they remain a bit skeptical about laymen like Cousins. Also, they are only gradually getting over their skepticism about hypnotherapy.

II

Sickness Is an Evil

Sister Claudia, a trained psychiatric
nurse, is in charge of the Chronic Pain
Unit in a large Catholic hospital

You are dealing with people always in pain but not terminally ill.
How does religion, or spirituality, help these patients?

It is not there specifically at the beginning of treatment.
The whole program is centered around the holistic approach
to health. Let me give you my basics. I feel that we are not
really created to be sick. I don't see sickness as a good at all;
it is an evil. The more I work with sick people, the more I am
convinced that illness is just one way of coping. We learn our
patterns of behavior when we are young, when we are threatened, or frightened, or insecure. We learn to protect ourselves in ways that seem to help at the time, by developing
patterns like shyness, procrastination, or hostility. It works
at first, and as time goes on those patterns become ingrained.

Youngsters are threatened by fear of failing in school, or
that somebody's going to laugh at them, anything that threatens their ego, anything that keeps us from being ourselves.
We are frightened even of being ourselves. Pretty soon these
patterns of behavior are so ingrained that we begin to think
that that's really us, but it isn't. I think that each one of us
was created marvelously, and each has his own internal blueprint to become himself. There is a blueprint inside of me that

my inner self knows. Nobody else knows. How I am going to become myself is to learn to be attentive to the signals that come from my emotions, my body, my spirit, and I must listen to the response. It's kind of like playing it by ear throughout life.

We don't pay attention to the signals we get from ourselves because that's the way we were brought up. You get out of bed in the morning and you feel a little bit down, so you just chug down three cups of coffee and you're ready to go. We override a lot of our feelings. For example, especially in the Christian tradition, we've been taught very effectively that anger is bad. So we are willing to stifle those feelings of anger and after a while we don't feel them anymore. We don't even know we are angry and we get all kinds of other symptoms instead. As a result, because we don't listen to ourselves, we are upset instead of being angry; we are off from the blueprint and we try to be other than we are. There's a lot of that in the American culture. The TV ads tell you what to buy to have social status, to get sex appeal, to have a fuller life. The big push is to be like everybody else. If we would just try to be ourselves, there wouldn't be that inner conflict that I really believe causes illness. I think that if we were really ourselves, we would not be sick, because there would be no conflict there.

I mean, of course, self-inflicted illness, but there's also the fact that a lot of people are accident prone. There's just no way out of it; some people get hit, and that's it. There are also human powers inside persons that we hardly use at all. Anyway, that's my basic premise about ourselves and health. If we really slowed down and listened and came in tune with who we are, we would be in pursuit of wholeness.

What is your professional training and education?

I got my bachelor's degree in nursing from a Jesuit university, became a registered nurse, and then took a master's in psychiatric nursing. But my philosophy of treatment really comes out of experience. I had eight years of nursing in two widely separated hospitals, at first in critical care and then in renal dialysis. Most of the time in the second hospital was in medical surgery and in the intensive care units. I was often frustrated because we were just treating patients to make them more comfortable. I had to struggle with periods of depression and sometimes I didn't want anything more to do with life, and that was more psychic pain than physical pain. It was an awful feeling. It's much more comfortable to be physically sick and it's also more acceptable to the people around you. If you're depressed they tell you right away to go see a psychiatrist. Fortunately I came through that experience and I can appreciate more readily what some of our pain patients suffer.

I think I had to put together my life as a sister and my life as a nurse to reach the concept of holistic health care. I always had a deep love of people, and I could feel myself reaching out to make patients more comfortable. I used to marvel that people could get well right there under your own fingertips. But I can also remember people not getting better who should have. Families and relatives would come in and you'd immediately sense the tension and I would think, well, it's no wonder this person is so sick. I recall taking care of a woman who had colitis and I was certain within myself that the colitis was psychosomatic. She was then celebrating her twenty-fifth wedding anniversary. They had been married in Hawaii and were going back to celebrate there. She couldn't go because she got sick. So they had to cancel the trip, and she started getting better. The rest of the family decided to wait for her recovery and then make the trip. As soon as she heard that, she got sick again. That was the first real suspicion I had that there is more to it than this medicine bit.

I began to realize that we were just treating the sickness as though it were something separate from the sick person. I thought that people weren't learning anything from their ulcers. We should be learning more about ourselves when we try to cure our illness. Then I read a book, *The Will To Live*, by Doctor Hutschnecker. He went through case after case and concluded that people not only choose their illness, but they choose when they are going to die. He claimed that we have that kind of control, and that's what really set me off. After that I read everything I could find by Paul Tournier, who is both religious and psychological and a medical doctor. The more I read the more frustrated I became because I felt that in nursing we were just touching the surface. We were just putting bandages on people until they came back to the hospital.

After coming to this hospital I was asked by the director of pastoral care and by our chief neurosurgeon to participate in the opening of this chronic pain unit. It has been in operation now for three years, and we continue to treat people who should not be in pain, or at least they should not have to continue carrying the burden of pain they bring in with them.

Many people complain to the physician who can find nothing physically wrong with them.

That may be as high as eighty percent of some doctors' patients. They usually are doctoring because they have hypertension, but that tension didn't come solely out of the blue. They've been building up to it for a long time, because they haven't been eating properly, haven't been expressing their feelings, haven't been in tune with their needs, haven't been listening to themselves. That's why they have hypertension. A person who drops dead of a heart attack had lots of signals that it was coming. That wasn't a shot out of the dark. There are a lot of things we ought to listen for. We just override them. Even people with cancer. We are learning more and more in the clinic now that cancer is clearly stress-related. People get cancer when they are really lonely and become alienated from themselves. You see it time and time again.

What I am saying is really hopeful talk. I think it's exciting because it shows there's a way out. We can learn new patterns of behavior to become more healthy. I can get to be in control of my health. If you believe that there's nothing you can do, if there's just fate, that's what scares you. What we need is to just kind of slow down and listen and relax. The people who come to this pain unit have chronic low back pain, and headaches, chest pains, and stomach pains. They've taken medication, they've had surgery, and nothing has helped. They may have had some temporary relief, but the pain always comes back, so they are usually very depressed and they don't have very much hope. Most of them have a medical history that shows where the pain began. They're not youngsters. Most of them are between forty and sixty. They usually have had an accident at work, or they fell down at home, or they had some kind of surgery. There was definitely a clear beginning of their pain to which you can trace it.

What is the treatment like?

A lot of what we do is to explain the holistic approach, how the mind and the body and the spirit all work together. To learn how to start reducing their pain, they're going to have to start to learn to understand the signals of their body. Pain is no more than a signal in these cases because there is nothing malignant going on here. It's a signal that they are doing something wrong, and we feel that if they do something differently maybe they can reduce their pain. We do an awful lot of relaxation training in that direction. Normally a person who is under stress tends to tighten up and to fight it, and if you are under stress for a long time, that breeds muscle tension, and the muscles will contract and become sore and tender. You don't have to have an accident if you are under tension and start to have headaches and your shoulders are going to become sore. But if you already have a body area that's vulnerable, say from an accident, then you get up-tight and those muscles clamp around that area that's already tender. You get more pain and you tighten up even more, and it's a vicious circle.

Tranquilizers are okay on a short term, but in the long run they are depressing. We teach them how to relax themselves without drugs. We take them down gradually and then they discover that they don't need them. They listen to the signals of their bodies and they let go. This is where I see the real connection between spirituality and what we are doing here. We're talking about a holistic approach, and the first meaning of holiness is to become whole. That's what Jesus was about. Religion is not separated from life, so that I do my God-thing over here and then live my life over there. Religion to be truly holy has to be whole. To me Jesus is the one who is the most whole. He came among us on earth and he went through hell. People hated him, he was under a lot of stress, but he never betrayed himself. There isn't any reported incident of Jesus getting sick. He knew what his limits were; he knew he was free to be compassionate and to be angry. He was in touch also with his healing. He had a lot of power and he was so whole because he was himself. If you teach a person to let go, to relax, I think it is a very religious experience, because if you let go it is a kind of trust.

Do you have to be a believer to say, "Relax, stop worrying"? Does God have to come into this?

I think that living this life demands a lot of faith, and people have to have faith in something. I don't think they'll make it otherwise. Maybe they'll get pretty far, but when it comes down to the crunch, they'll fall on their faces without the Lord. We must realize too that it's not just mind over matter, or a kind of self-hypnosis. It's a real physical change that occurs. Muscles are relaxing, the aggravation of the pain lessens. It's not just a mental deal. That is what biofeedback is all about. It measures physical changes in the contractions of the muscles. People often come in here with the mistaken notion that "you're going to teach me how to live with my pain." We tell them, "No, we are going to help you to learn how to reduce the pain." Some people can reduce it completely. Others can't, but they can learn to get down to a certain level, to a point where pain is not controlling their lives.

The spiritual dimension makes sense to me in my own mind, and that's how I relate it to people when they ask me for an explanation. Right now we are trying to bring in a program that is definitely more spiritual. But we've been a little cautious because some people get religion all screwed up and are very superstitious about magic powers. They hang on to their mixed-up notions about religion and I sometimes think they are worse than the people who don't believe anything. What we are working on now is to have a period each day just to pray together, and to pray for healing. We haven't done that yet. Our patients may attend the daily Mass in the hospital chapel if they wish. Hardly any of them do.

Religion can become a crutch, and from one point of view I can understand that. I am cautious about bringing religion and spiritual matters to the people in pain because they get mixed up about it. I'm a professed religious but it has taken me a long time to get myself in balance on this, and I feel good about the way I believe. But most people I talk to who haven't had a good religious training don't have religion integrated into their lives. So you take a risk when you talk about religious beliefs. People interpret you within their own framework, and they get it all wrong. They take off on a weird tangent that you never intended. Usually they put all the responsibility on God when there is a very fine line between trusting in God completely and yet being responsible for yourself. When I say trust God, he's not asking me to be passive and he's not asking me to be controlled either. Powerlessness is very significant and I really don't know how to define it.

There are non-believers too who say you cause your own illness.

That's right. I know that religion is really integrated in my own life. I don't know how other people can do it without a solid belief in the Lord and what he is saying. Somewhere down the line, if you keep going through these rough spots, you're going to land face to face with Jesus. Whether you know him or not, I think it's the same road. Whether you believe in Jesus or not, if you stay on that same road you will meet him. I really think he is there, and I don't know how you could do it without him. You can pass up some things when you get into a crisis situation, and you may say, "Those are just the breaks," but sooner or later you realize that you can't do it on your own. In real tragedies, when everything is falling apart, you've got to have faith; you've got to believe.

It's at those times, I think, you are going to meet the Lord even if you did not know him before.

After all, the Muslims and the Jews believe in God, and that's what Jesus was talking about. His whole message was about the Father, and they believe in him whether they call him Yahweh, or Allah, or Buddha. I am not sure that Jesus really cares how you get there in touch with God. I am not saying that all religions are the same, or that one is as good as another. I think we have an advantage, of course, in knowing Jesus, and that puts us a hundred years ahead.

You give me the impression you need intelligence to get well. Does the patient have to be smart to get cured at this pain clinic?

I don't think so, but you really have to want to get well, and you don't have to be able to articulate these beliefs. Most of us are not willing to work toward wholeness because it's very hard to do. We don't want to take the risk of being different from everybody else. That's also painful. We would rather suffer with our headaches even though we don't make that choice consciously. There are other things that are more important to us than the stress we suffer. A woman may think it's more important to retain her husband's respect than to acknowledge to herself and reveal to him that he is the source of her distress.

Tell me a little about the structure of the program.

Well, our capacity is an even dozen who usually come in as a group—although we will receive a single individual if there is room—and we keep them for four weeks. The majority are female, and that's quite typical. More females than males enter the health care system because women are more inclined to allow themselves to be sick and to seek help when they are sick.

Let me say that the chaplain who runs the pastoral care department at the hospital comes up with every new group and gives them a talk about spirituality and religion, that it's holistic and it doesn't specifically focus on Christians. We deal with anybody who's in pain. They like to talk with him. Then our chief neurosurgeon comes in to give a bit of history and an explanation of our existence. Everyone with chronic pain, as a last resort, goes to a neurosurgeon because they figure he can cut a nerve or something like that and stop the pain. The surgeons are the ones who see all the failures of the medical system to take care of chronic pain.

To get this unit going he got a biofeedback machine and hired an assistant. They went to a couple of workshops and were doing this on a part-time basis on the seventh floor where some patients were in pain and others were not. They weren't satisfied, and when this space was available they moved the program down here. That's when I came with it. We were giving physical therapy to each person every day; we were using stimulators, but not many of them had bio-feedback. The program only gradually became formalized. It's a multi-disciplinary program and that includes anaesthe-siologist, neurosurgeon, social worker, psychiatrist, nurses, physical therapist, and occupational therapist. When it comes right down to the crunch it's the nurses who hold it together and the others come in as needed. I'd like to see it really more integrated than it is.

You don't mention pastoral ministry among the multi-disciplines.

There are two reasons, and everybody knows this is a Catholic hospital. The first is that the chaplains from the hos-pital are part-time in this unit. The second is that the whole team is made up of people who understand professionally the role of religion in health care. One of our really saintly people is a biofeedback therapist who has a master's degree and counsels them spiritually and prays with them. She works a lot with out-patients who are not on the regular four-week program who suffer migraine headaches, or have Rey-naud's disease. That's a vascular disorder where the hands get very cold and the fingertips turn blue. She works with them on a one-to-one basis and doesn't concentrate on the whole group as I do.

What is the daily schedule for the patient group?

During the first week we get them gradually into the swing of things, explaining our philosophy of well-being even if they don't always remember it. They get a grasp of the holistic notion, that it's all integrated, how it all links together. We give them a good chance to reduce their muscle tension, how to relax. We tell them that pain is a message to be understood, not to be fought. We have good group discussions on this. Twice a day they go down for physical therapy. Every day we have them play biofeedback and relaxation tapes. One set of discussions is about moods, what they are, how they control your life, and what to do about them. In a way it's like a short course in psychology. Another discussion focuses on means of physical fitness, nutrition and exercise, hygiene and sleep, just understanding your body and how it works. We talk about emotional health, being in tune with your feelings, expressing yourself, communicating better, being assertive.

Meanwhile, you're taking all their pills away.

We do that gradually but we tell them right in the beginning, and they all want to get rid of them. Most of the time their pain medication wasn't helping them anyway. Sometimes after we get them off their pain medication they say that they still hurt but that the pain is no worse than it was. In fact, it may be one-tenth of what it was when they were on pills. You get them on Tylenol, and even after they are home a year ninety percent are still on Tylenol and have not gone back to anything narcotic. We try to help them increase their self-awareness and their activities so they're not just moping around and driving everyone crazy. Our goal for them is to start to live again. You can see it in their eyes. When they first come in they are depressed, the pain's got them down, and they can't even focus. By the time they go home you can also see it in their eyes that they have regained hope. But they have to be motivated. It's much easier to take a pill or to find somebody who'll do surgery on you, or to keep hunting for the panacea. This is a tough program, and you may be surprised that most of them stay with it and succeed. Even sometimes when they do poorly they may go through some kind of crisis six months later, and then they turn around and are okay.

Do you have a follow-up after they leave here?

Yes, we keep contact for about a year if they want that. We check with them in about three weeks and again at six weeks, mainly to encourage them. Then we wait for about six months, but they can call us in the meantime and check back all during the year. The spiritual dimension has to continue in importance, and I sometimes suggest to those leaving here that they go to one of the prayer groups, pentecostal or charismatic, that strongly believes in the healing power of God in their lives. By this time I think they've got the message and won't misinterpret it.

III

Listening for Pain

Father Donald, a Jesuit psychiatrist,
teaches at a university medical school
and treats patients in a 1,100-bed hospital

*You are teaching students how to deal with people in pain. Tell me
how you do that.*

Trying to focus on pain means for me to get the medical
student, the nurse, the chaplain, to listen to what a person
says. The things I have a hard time getting students to listen
to are the same issues that all people cannot listen to. These
are the things that upset us, or that hurt us, or that inflict a
threat or sometimes psychic pain on us. An example would
be the patient who says, "I just don't like the thought of having to go off and leave my three small children." Now the person who hears that comment—if he has any maturity at all—
realizes that he doesn't have an answer for that. There is no
facile response, and yet he may feel tongue-tied, or may want
to avoid the topic, or may want to get into something else.

From my viewpoint I think you can help them if you listen to anything else they want to say about that. You might
say something like, "It's hard to imagine having to face that."
Or you might even ask them, "How do you do it?" That's a
question I repeatedly ask people and they will tell me all the
things they have sustained during their lives or in the short

period of time in their illness. I say to them, "That strikes me; and the way you put it, it's almost overwhelming. How do you cope with that?" I am curious about what they use to bear pain. They may not give me very much, and just say "I get by," but I want to know "How?" It's a kind of sensitivity about not wanting to intrude but at the same time in a gentle way you're wanting to know if they can tell you. My point with the medical students, or with any other professional group, is that these patients are the experts. You don't have a program with them. When they tell you something, you should treat it as though you found a gold mine.

Why is it so difficult for the patient to talk?

Well, first of all, nobody wants to hear them because that's very painful. They think the mother is going to break down now if she says she's going to die before her children ever come of age. You think you should stop her from talking about that, because who wants her to break down? You really don't know whether or not the mother wants to talk about that. Health care personnel have these difficulties. If the patient tries to talk about it they say, "There, there, it'll be O.K.," or "Now, now, don't cry." And, of course, the sick person's view is, "Well, O.K., if they can't take it, I won't talk about it." It is good for them to talk about it, if that's what they want to do. The obligation of the health care person is that you have to be brave enough to hear it.

I'll give you an example. I had this woman patient in front of the class who said quietly, "Well, I have this tumor and I've thought about death," and I'll say, "Does that frighten you?" She says, "Not really, because death is final." You ask her, "Is there nothing afterward?" and she says, "Oh, this is a thing in my family. I talked to my mother about it." Then I just keep talking with that lady about her view of death—not about mine—and where she gets those ideas. After she leaves we have a class discussion, and someone in the audience is very likely to get up and say: "That woman is a liar." They are very angry at her, and their point is that nobody could be that calm about death unless one had religious faith. All I'm saying is that the person who makes that kind of comment has a problem of insecurity about his own faith. He can't tolerate hearing someone express a different view and say it with calmness.

How does the patient help you find a solution?

You can't find a solution by refusing to listen or by immediately contradicting the patient. I hold these seminars every other week, open to anyone associated with the hospital staff. We get seminarians and nurses and interns. I invite the patient to tell us what it's like to be sick. I want them to hear that, but they will not listen. Because they won't listen they don't ask simple questions to find out what the patients are like, that they are real people and not just "the patient with the metastatic pancreatic cancer."

After we interview a woman who is terminally ill somebody will say, "Well, the trouble with her is that she just doesn't know enough," and then they go into their own little solution about bearing the cross of pain. The fact that they get so upset about somebody who has a different perspective means that they are insecure themselves. My point is that if we have any honesty about us we should be willing to know that God may speak to individuals in ways that we are unfamiliar with, and we ought to be willing to hear that. I find that most of us are unwilling to listen.

I may get into a conversation with a lady who says, "Oh, I love to pray to St. Anthony." Now my job is to find out about that, and I ask: "What's the relationship between St. Anthony and God?" But at the time I start to talk about St. Anthony the Catholics in the audience are getting restless. They are shifting around in their seats. They think St. Anthony is a superstition. They think she ought to be reading Schillebeeckx. What I'm saying is that you listen to that lady and you hear how God talks to her. I'll ask her, "Who's first, St. Anthony or God?" That's an honest question, and she'll say, "Well, God, of course." For me that's a wonderful thing to hear. I really am charmed by what people say. I think their theology is quite profound if people will listen to it. But now they won't because they are so wedded to their own theoretical formulations; they are unwilling to hear what the relationship is of the person to God.

Why do seminarians come to your open meetings?

For some of them it's what they call field work; and some of them are going to be hospital chaplains. The nurses are there because they know they will have to talk to sick people. But they are all worried that the patients are going to talk about their illness, and death, and separation from family. Most of them are really uptight that the patient will talk about religious faith. The nurses will usually say, "That's not our job to talk about faith." Even so, they are sure they have to offer the patients something about God, as though the patient never knew anything at all about God. That's the folly of rushing in as though we have this great thing to offer them, and we are going to lay it on them.

I tell the seminarians: "Save yourself first. You have nothing to offer, but if you listen to what the patient has to teach you, you will do him a big favor, and you will learn something yourself. The patient will teach you several things. First, what it's like to be sick. Second, maybe there are some ways to cope with it so that if you ever get that sick you don't have to despair. You can use these people as models and as edifying examples. Remember that and you won't be so scared when you get sick. Third, you can really ask the challenging questions like: Does God talk to people on an inner level or not? Is all that stuff about religious belief just a myth?"

Medical and nursing students don't plan to bring in the Bible, but they have to be concerned about the patient's emotional well-being. Can they cope with death? What does it mean to them? How are they going to take it? If so, how can they as health care experts help the patients? They have to decide too whether religion is a helpful thing. What should they do for the person? Should they talk up religion, encourage them to go back to church, or are they just supposed to call the chaplain and let him handle it? A lot depends on the willingness of the individual medical student to say, "If I were in those straits what would I do?" A lot of them won't listen because they don't want to think of themselves ever in those straits.

You can notice that the younger a patient is on the ward the more upset the staff is likely to be. The young mother age twenty-nine is a terribly threatening person to have for young nurses because they identify with her. Nobody wants that. They think, "It will never happen to me." Yet all around them the sick people are a reminder that it can. They don't even say, "How will I cope with it?" They don't say: "Is God going to be with me or not? Is God with these people or not?" They are so threatened and I just want to take the threat away, and get them to be curious and to listen to these people. If anybody copes with it, if anybody is getting any support from God, here is your chance to find out. If you think you are going to find it in books, I just don't believe that you can.

Are you suggesting that these sick people have found a way to cope with their pain?

Given the amount of pain and the amount of loss, separation and distress, I would say that their ability to cope with it has been absolutely edifying. I've never been so impressed as I have been with people in those circumstances. Now, you've got different kinds of pain patients. If you look at people who have cancer and have pain on that basis, that's one group. If you look at people who are chronic pain patients, who are in pain clinics, they are quite a different group. They are not so edifying for the most part. The reasons for their being in the chronic pain clinic are not clear. The doctors who have been looking at these people don't understand why they are in so much pain because it seems to be out of all proportion to the objective findings. Those people are not edifying to me. They are not terminal and they have a lot of psychological problems. They are game-players. Some are depressed and their depression can be treated. Very few of these people have an honest relationship with God. I have questioned them.

Of course, I'm generalizing and I don't mean to say that everybody who has chronic pain is a phony. These are people who have pain, and they have a problem. They come there and they want somebody to work it up. There is a sub-group of those people, however, who've been not only to your pain clinic but also to other pain clinics. They may have had surgery several times and they present themselves and say, "Oh, doctor, I came to your clinic because you can heal everything. I know. I put all my trust in you." That is really a personality type as far as I'm concerned, and the pain there functions as some kind of communication, or in place of honest communication.

We keep using the word "pain," but I guess I think more of the word "suffering." Where I work, in a very large general hospital, severe pain is usually a somewhat transient phenomenon. If you have a cancer patient, for example, ninety percent of the pain can be controlled. But there are many forms of suffering that are much worse, the worst being abandonment, or separation. The pain clinic patients have many forms of human anguish that are interpersonal. They need psychiatric help to get over that, and it's very complicated. I myself do not warm to those people. Their interpersonal relations are often distorted and they are not like somebody who makes an honest request for help. You try to help and you try to be honest with them. You go back and forth, and you do what you can. That doesn't happen with the average chronic pain patient who's been in the pain clinic and keeps coming back. There is a lot of interpersonal difficulty based on psychological sickness. They are not appealing. They don't edify me.

I interviewed in a pain clinic where the neurosurgeon allows no place for spiritual input. That surprises me.

It does me too. Of course, it could be a very depressing job. There is one very valuable question for a chaplain to ask in a place like that. You listen to their story and you ask them, "Where does God stand in all this?" From my point of view, the answer is a crucial one. It tells me what they think about

God. I want to know, "Does God want you to have this?"
Some people will say, "You know, God chastises me. It
makes up for the sinful lives of other people." If people say
that, they're masochists; they're sick, I think, and have a poor
relationship with God. How could you love that kind of God?
I said to another man who is dying of stomach cancer, "All
the things you describe to me, I don't see how you can take
them. Where does God stand in all this?" He said, "Well, he's
a nice old man. You know, the world is going to hell but he
does the best he can." Now, that man has a good relationship
with God. There is something about that contact that is
wholesome. I think if a chaplain were to ask in a chronic pain
clinic "Where does God stand in all this?" he would get some
of the most distorted answers.

Maybe these are exceptional cases, but there are too
many of them. I see a lot of people with metastatic cancer
whose pain is sort of fluctuating and manageable. They are
not going back and forth from place to place asking, "What
can we do about it?" They have an adequate and acceptable
form of control even though they do have chronic pain. They
do their best to cope. Now these are exceptional or extraordinary people. Our neurosurgeon can help maybe one-fourth
to one-third of them. The rest are typical repeaters.

This woman, for example, comes in to our neurosurgeon
and she has this terrible pain. Her own neurosurgeon has run
three operations and is thinking about a fourth, but he feels
that the fourth one could be very serious. So he sends her up
to our doctor to evaluate her, because he is not sure what the
objective reason is for all this pain. The psychiatrist interviews her and learns that she is having an affair with the neurosurgeon who operated on her three times, and he is about
to get rid of her. Of course, she is crying, "Pain, pain, pain,"
as though she's saying, "You can't let me go now." What are
you going to do with that? As a good intervener he could say,
"Maybe some of your intensified pain is due to this." She was
a reasonable lady and she said, "Well, you know, that may
be right." That kind of thing is more commonly found in a
chronic pain clinic, and it's very difficult to handle. The chaplain could be helpful if he came in just to keep people honest.

What is the function of the chaplain with people in pain?

The chaplain is a sacrament, and if you think about that, he is a sacrament of God's healing presence in some way. When you have someone with an incurable problem, whether it's a disease or a pain, I think that the chaplain stands there to be present, as God is present, in a supportive strengthening way. That's the way he is with his personal presence. How does he develop it, and what do they expect? The patients expect spiritual competence from this man as a chaplain. If you wear a badge and it says "chaplain" it means that you have some special expertise in relating to God. So he delves into the patient's personal relationship with God. He cannot immediately intervene. He has to find out what it is like. They'll tell him, "Well, of course, I was a hell-raiser. I ran amuck in the service and I got syphilis bad. That's why I have this prostatic cancer and I bleed, and I have all this bone pain." Then he has to figure out why he thinks God would be so punitive to him and what he knows about God. So it's an effort to get the person in touch with God's presence. There are people who go to chronic pain clinics who resist normal relationships with human beings, and they will do the same with God. They really don't want somebody who is kind and considerate with them.

The chaplain has to be aggressive. Listening is not passive. When the patient says, "I imagine this is because I've sown some wild oats in my time," the priest responds, "You mean that God is putting this on you because of those wild oats?" Now, you've got to get to that and not simply assume that he thinks like that. He's not ready for a lecture. Anybody who would give him a lecture at that point is a fool. It's just like saying that you don't want to hear his story. The priest should ask, "Do you mean to say that's how you see God?" and he should be curious about that. Then he might ask, "Do you think God is a sadist?" He's going to ask those questions and he's not going to rest until he finds out how the patient formulates his idea of what God is like. I'm not going to project my own thing on him. I'm not going to say to the person,

"God isn't like that." Certainly not at that point because I tell you it won't do any good.

For example, the patient will feel very guilty about saying to himself, "God is a bloody butcher." Now he feels guilty. He's balking at God and he's cursing him, but he's not going to say that. You tell him, "Now, wait a minute. Your logic says that you're bleeding and you're dying from this disease that God gave you because back in wartime you did some of these things. What kind of a person would do that to you?" He will start to hem and haw, and then you can ask: "Is that because you have a kind of harsh picture of God?" Now, if you can get him to spell out that picture, then you've got him where you want him. You can start talking to him about the scriptures which say this lady was supposed to be stoned for adultery and Jesus didn't do anything about that. If the patient didn't admit what he thought, namely, that this was a sadistic brutal punishment—which is a very important thing to help him say—you are not going to get anyplace on that.

Are you saying that some chaplains talk too much?

That's right, and if patients can't talk with you, don't push them. If the person is gasping for breath while you are trying to get this clinical interview down, well you shouldn't be in the ministry in the first place. I guess I'm talking about an ideal setup where you can find out what people think about God. There are other principles, like putting your hands on people. Touch is one of the sacramentals we've always known about. You are trying to understand what people's feelings are. You can't do that unless you are brave enough to say, "Well, how would I feel if I were in that situation?" If you are brave enough, then the prayer you articulate will be much more moving. If you are hurt by their pain, then they will know that. If you have a kind of breezy style and you tell them, "Now, keep a stiff upper lip; that's good," that saves you, but they don't feel that there is somebody now who really understands. You want them to get that because you would like them to think that God understands them. God is present to them, and therefore when they are feeling bad God might hold them. It means you have to be a *Mensch*. You can tell them about yourself, and in that way you are becoming a person to them. Those are the things I hope a chaplain would do by instinct.

All I am saying is that you have to take the spiritual temperature of the person. The benefit of being a regular chaplain in one place is that you can learn a little bit at a time more things about the person without trying to overwhelm him all at once. We can't sell short the complex relationship that God has with an individual. I think it's a mystery but we have to treat it as a goal. Some people think the main thing is to get over all the preliminaries fast and then give them the truth. I am saying that if they can inform you about how God relates to them, you will soon have a book on how good God is to his people—how he manifests himself, and how he keeps people close to him, how he's there all the time, and that you are not such a big almighty figure of a chaplain. You're not there to dispense the word of God. God is already there and you are there to be a sacrament of God's presence.

An awful lot of physicians won't say that God is already there.

But I do say it as a physician. Some of these doctors say, "I don't understand anything about religion," and I'll say, "Why don't you ask the patients?" If you want to know whether religion does any good for them, why don't you ask them, because the patients have a way of making believers out of people. What I know from my own experience is that they strengthen my belief. They tell me about the way God touches them, and I'm saying to myself, "Oh my God, this is something special." It's that little phrase in Saint Paul, "Faith speaks to faith." If you want your faith to grow, or to be nurtured, you can just listen to the patients, and it's a very impressive thing.

I am sure that most people have a relationship with God. I've had the chance to interview people who say they are agnostics. They'll talk to me about death, and I ask them if they are frightened. They say, "No," and one of my favorite questions then is, "Is there anything after death?" Sometimes they hedge their bets in some way and I begin to have a clue that something is going on here. If they say they are agnostic I'll ask them about their history and tradition. They'll tell me about their parents and their early years. The seminarians who visit the patients in the chronic disease hospital find a lot of crypto-believers who actually admit that they have some thoughts of God. They had had strong denominational ties that they wouldn't tell anybody about. They were mad at organized religion, and the chaplain to them really represents organized religion, so they clam up.

IV

God and the Handicapped

Sister Stephanie is the interdenominational chaplain of a municipal hospital for the rehabilitation of the
handicapped

*What is your background and training for the position you hold in
this public hospital?*

I have two academic graduate degrees in counseling, and
my first assignment as a sister was as guidance counselor in
a Catholic girls' high school. Seven years ago I took the four
units of Clinical Pastoral Education training with a Baptist
minister supervisor who is a very religious man. The archdiocese pays for chaplains in six of the non-Catholic hospitals, so I was hired to work half-time here and half-time at a
much larger public hospital.

They took me on first as a kind of trainee, and I didn't
realize till later that it was a year of tryout and probation. The
administration and staff had earlier been very opposed to
having a chaplain of any kind at this city hospital. Their experience had been with ministers and clergymen coming in
and telling the people that if they prayed enough they would
get better, and not really understanding the process of rehabilitation. But the day came when the administrator here
talked with the chaplain supervisor at City General Hospital

and said he was ready to hire a chaplain and would be willing to take me on if I continued my training while here. That's why I call it a year's probation.

Is there a disadvantage in being a woman on this job?

Yes, it was very difficult. When I was first hired I met a lot of resistance here, mainly because they hired a Catholic and secondly because they hired a woman. I don't know which was worse. The administrator I report to was raised a Catholic. He told me on the very day I was hired, "I had nothing to say in this, and I am opposed to it." In time that has changed with him, but there are some who say they prefer a man. Nowadays I don't think a sister would get that kind of flak at a church-related hospital.

Many of us are not fortunate enough to work in a Catholic-run hospital, and we have a harder battle. We have to prove that we are needed here and that we are of value. When I came down the hall just now this nurse said to me, "I'm glad you're back. This place needs you badly." That was five years of hard work to get this kind of recognition, and to get doctors and the staff and administrators to say "we really need a chaplain here." I was the first permanent one they hired, and they tell me now that if I were to leave, this hospital would hire another chaplain. It's very different at your church-affiliated hospitals that are really committed to pastoral care. When I go to the Catholic chaplains' meetings here in the city, I always tell them they don't know what it is to have to struggle to prove yourself. Catholic hospitals take it for granted. They believe in it. Here you have to prove it to them.

One of the advantages in my favor is that I now have double certification in pastoral care. After getting the rigorous training in CPE I made application to the Catholic group. On the strength of my professional status all I had to do was write a paper and then I was certified by the Office of Chaplain Services. I am probably unique in being an approved supervisor who can train pastoral care students in both systems.

Is there much difference between the two?

Basically, the difference is that the Catholic training includes so many hours of theology and other academic subjects that you must cover. The program of Clinical Pastoral Education has much less intellectual input and doesn't have that kind of formal routine. I am not sure I will want to renew my CPE supervising status when it comes up this autumn. I may hold off for a while. One of my problems with CPE all along has been that they are very clinical minded. Some of the supervisors in this area do a great deal with transactional analysis.

I think the history of CPE started with Anton Boisen who had a mental breakdown, but we have moved beyond what he originally wanted to do. One of the problems was that the clergyman came into the sick room and moved right away to the spiritual, and that was all done in the head; the clergyman didn't really know where the person was. CPE tried to counteract that by teaching counseling techniques but never really got back to the spiritual dimensions. I think that some of that is changing, and that many of the CPE supervisors in this area now know that if we want to touch people's lives and bring Christ to them we must first touch them where they are hurting.

Do you postpone the spiritual until you do the psychological?

That's not quite the way to say it. If you do not teach basic counseling skills and listening skills, then they go in and give the patient a lot of religious talk. I found my students quoting scripture to the patients, talking to them a lot. Later, when I asked them "What was the matter with that patient? What was wrong?" they couldn't say because they didn't know. Sometimes that's what happens when you have a basic unit of beginners who are well intentioned and zealous but the counseling skills and the listening skills are just not there. After you learn how to get in touch with that person then you do the thing you are really trained to do. You've got the theological content that is essential for pastoral care.

At one of the national conventions of ACPE they invited Henri Nouwen who is very strong on getting back to the roots of the spiritual dimension. I think he made his point and the ACPE people in general are really trying to come back to this, but they continue to emphasize the psychological over the spiritual, and they don't provide sufficient theological insights in their training units. I'm on several committees in the ACPE, and I find in my committee work that they have a hangup about chaplains who don't get married. With all their psychology they still have no clear understanding of celibacy. This seems symptomatic of a general misunderstanding of the wide dimensions of the spiritual life.

How long does it take to bring God into the conversation?

I think we can get into that very rapidly through asking such questions as "Where is God for you right now?" As I listen to patients talk I frequently say, "Tell me about your God." I think it's important for me to have that clarified where God is, or what kind of a God they have, and where their relationship with God is. I often find with sick people that they feel that God has abandoned them. Their feelings are so strong about what has happened to them they don't admit it is they who moved away from God. And often they can be brought to recognize that. The fears, the anxieties, the feelings, and maybe the anger about what happened to them has blocked them from recognizing that God was really in their life.

A second thing that is important for me is that at a time of sickness, people sort of reexamine what kind of God they have. Isn't that what Ignatius Loyola did when he was laid up in bed? I always refer to a time of sickness as similar to retreat time. People can use hospital time as retreat time, when they reexamine God and their relationship with God, and they reexamine what the church has meant to them.

But they also want to know, "Why did God do this to me?"

I don't believe there is any answer to that. I ultimately try to turn it around and ask, "What can I do with what has happened to me?" In this case, particularly with the handicapped, I have to say, "I don't know why you are paralyzed. But the more important question is: What can you do with your life now? How can you make it more meaningful? How can you make it come closer to God?" As I reexamine my values I have to change my life-style. One thing I am sure about is that God intends that suffering bring us closer to him, and not take us away from him.

It's not easy to give a clear answer when you're dealing with the suffering of handicapped and disabled people. How can we use suffering for the purpose that God intended it to be used? That's a basic question we each have to answer for ourselves. I see a lot of people turning bitter and losing their faith. That's very common with the handicapped people; they just totally give up faith. Many of my former patients now say that they are agnostics, or that they are atheists. I know I am not making it clear, but I feel very challenged to say that we all have to find that in our own lives. Just last week I buried a very close friend who suffered intensely before she died. I spent a lot of time with this friend, and I ended up seeing life and death more seriously than before. There's also been a lot of illness in my family. Those are all sufferings in my own life.

How can I come closer to God, and how can I get other people to do that? I think that as a whole we are more inclined to become angry over it and to block it off. For the first time I said last week, "I know why people lose their faith," but I know that people don't have to lose their faith. Maybe they need somebody. I think that one of the things that happens to people in hospitals and people in sickness is that they feel very alone. They feel very alienated. Many of our patients say to me, "My previous idea of clergymen was that they were people who came in and told you what to do, but never tried to understand you." So it is important in my pastoral work that they feel that I do understand them and want to be close to them. Then I think the door is open for grace to work in and through them.

The ascetical writers say that Jesus suffered to redeem us from our sins, which seems to mean that sin is somehow connected with suffering.

Perhaps we have to end up by saying that pain is a mystery. I attended John Powell's workshop, and I feel that his core concept could be used with sick people and very much with the handicapped. What can I do with my reality? He taught us how to do a lot of things with what is going on inside of ourselves. The whole idea is that I can choose to be a happy person, or I can choose to be an unhappy person, and that's a big choice. But I want to look at the things I am doing that are misconceptions, or that are false. He taught us to trigger our wrong thinking with counter-thinking or counter-logic. But he also said, "We have to accept pain as a condition of existence." I need to study that. I came back from the workshop to get right into this situation where my friend was dying, and I didn't have much time to do anything about it. Jesus didn't do away with his own suffering, but he had an attitude toward it. My attitude will bring about the feelings I have, and it is within my power to change my attitudes.

What are the medical doctors' attitudes toward your work?

They are much more cooperative than they used to be. I have a unique advantage here in that we have only ten doctors on the medical staff. When our patients arrive here they are placed under the care of one of our doctors. When they are discharged they go back to their own doctor. In contrast, the public city hospital has about four hundred doctors. Here I have a chance to get to know the doctors, and I find that due to the kind of work you do with patients, doctors become educated to what you can do. When a new doctor first comes in he may make a referral like this: "This is a religious man; would you see him?" As the doctor gets to know me and my work he will say, "This patient is a difficult patient, Chaplain. Would you go in and see him?" or he'll say, "This patient has no family. His wife deserted him. Would you go in and talk with him?" So it's a matter of working closely with doctors. I also have the unique opportunity here that every morning the doctors sit down with their staff and discuss their patients, and I am always in on those meetings. So, in the course of a five-day week, I have been at a meeting with every doctor, discussing his patients.

It is very unusual for a hospital chaplain, but once you are hired by this hospital you are a staff member with a genuine professional commitment. It's not quite the flexible arrangement you tend to find in Catholic hospitals, and I think those chaplains wouldn't want the job here because of such disadvantages. For instance, you have to keep your certain hours, and you have to fill in a time sheet. We had a priest over at the city hospital who came in at ten o'clock and walked out every day at three o'clock. He seemed to have no idea of professional commitment. Well, I can't do that here. A lot of chaplains feel also that if you get hired by a public hospital you are going to be doing a lot of clerical work. I'm not. I fill in an approximation of how many patients I see every month and turn it in to my administrator, and that's all the paper work I have to do.

Another thing is that I attend the department head meetings. We have a department directors' luncheon once a month, and I'm active in those discussions. I'm on any committee I choose to join, like the patient-education committee. We have an ethics committee that is being formed right now, and I'm on it. It's very clear that the pastoral care department here is an integral part of the hospital and is meant to make a genuine contribution to health care and rehabilitation of patients. So, if you are hired by the hospital you have a chance to influence people.

Are you the only chaplain here in pastoral care?

Yes, officially and as staff member, but we do have some who come in part-time. My only frustration here is that there is not enough time to spend with each patient. You see, this is not like an in-and-out acute care facility. Crippled and handicapped people tend to stay here for a long time. I concentrate on them when they first come in. After they are here for two or three weeks they are on a full schedule and it's very difficult for me to get to see them. They are not scheduled for spiritual ministry by the chaplain as they are scheduled for other services. They are in activities all day long. We might have a paraplegic here for three months' treatment. When he is first here it is very easy for me to see him, but as his treatment nears the end he's in a full program all day long.

On the average we have been running about 115 patients right now. Unfortunately, we had closed a whole floor because of lack of doctors. We intend soon to open that floor so that actually we could have a capacity of 185 patients. The fact is that I can't really handle the number of patients we have right now, and I'd like to see one chaplain on every floor. I'm sure we'll never see that. That will never happen. That would be a ratio of one chaplain to about forty people. You can't even do a good job at that because if you are going to work with the handicapped you've also got to work with their families.

You get along well with the doctors. Tell me about the nurses.

Nurses are my prime people here. When I got back from furlough they were ready to tell me all about the patients and the patients' needs. The nurses are my most valuable source of referral and information. The nurses know a great deal more than the doctors about the patient as a human being, and it really helps me to get their insights and comments about the patient's well-being.

Do you find nurses praying with people?

No, but it's interesting that you should ask that. That's what happens in a Catholic hospital. I don't think that in this public hospital either the nurses or the patients expect prayer. Of course, with me it's probably expected. Patients generally will say, "Chaplain, will you pray for me?" And I often say, "Why don't we pray together?" and they say, "Oh, but Chaplain, I don't know how to pray." The fact is that by praying together I can help teach people how to pray because

I take the very things that we had been talking about and turn them into a prayer. It becomes a conversation with God, and they learn how to bring their concerns to Jesus. I think prayer is an essential part of all that.

Have you seen any miracles of healing?

I haven't seen anything like that happen that could be associated with faith or prayers. I have seen a situation where the doctor will say, "I did not expect that to happen," and it did happen. We had a patient walk out of here who was never expected to walk again. It seems to me that that's very common in the medical field. Maybe the same thing would be called a miracle if it happened after you had prayed for it. But here is something that happens for which no one prayed to God, no faith was involved, and the person gets better. Now the doctor can say, "Well, we don't claim to know everything; therefore, we don't know why this happened," but he does not have to say it's an intervention by God.

One of our sisters was in the hospital back home in an advanced stage of Hodgkin's disease. The chaplain brought in a woman to pray over her, a charismatic who laid hands on sister and told her she would be healed. She was in the fourth stage of the disease, which is the final stage, but now she is up and around again. She has been back down here to the hospital for tests and the doctors could not find anything wrong with her, no evidence of Hodgkin's disease.

As a final question: Are there many other sisters in your congregation who are in pastoral care?

We have a lot of sisters who would like to do this, but they can't get jobs. There is also a real need for hospital chaplains, but there isn't any money. The archdiocese pays the salaries for six sisters to do pastoral care in non-Catholic hospitals, but is not increasing that number. Many public hospitals simply don't budget for chaplains. They could use one percent of what they get from Blue Cross to pay for chaplains, but they also have other uses to which they want to put that money. Mercy sisters can get jobs in their own Mercy hospitals, but my community doesn't have any hospitals so we don't have very many options. That's why in my community the sisters are not going into it, but there is a great deal of interest in this work.

There's another aspect in this for women religious. If a hospital is willing to hire a Catholic chaplain they won't hire a sister because she can't do the whole sacramental ministry. You see, I wasn't hired here as a Catholic chaplain. I was hired as an interdenominational chaplain. I've been checking the want ads for hospitals, and I could not apply as a Catholic chaplain because I can't fulfill all the requirements. Notice the different wording: when the ad says "pastoral associate" they are looking for a sister. A public hospital advertising for a Catholic chaplain will word the ad, "able to fulfill all the obligations," and that's a way to get around saying "priest."

V

Charismatic Healing

Doctor Vincent, active in the Catholic
charismatic renewal, is a specialist in
surgery of the head and neck

Do you recognize a Christian response to pain and suffering?

I am certain that we ought to have a Christian approach
to everything we do, and especially in our professional life. I
personally haven't clearly defined it for the kind of surgery I
do or really thought much about it. From my reading of scripture and other studies, like Morton Kelsey's *Healing and Christianity*, and Frank MacNutt's best-sellers about the ministry
of healing, I say that God's general will is for people to be
healed. Primarily, of course, my approach is to do the very
best I can medically. If a patient is open to be prayed with, or
asks to pray, I am happy to do that with him or her.

As a general rule when we do offer a prayer, the request
comes from the patient, but it depends on the person and the
circumstances. If someone comes here, for instance, who is
involved in the Catholic charismatic renewal, or in the As-
sembly of God, or like the lady who came in this morning
who is from the Word of Faith Temple, these are the people
I know are open to be prayed with, but at the same time I'm
not running a prayer meeting in my office. I don't offer to
pray with just everyone who walks in the office. I am not interested in turning people off.

What kind of prayer do you say with them?

You know how we pray in the renewal, spontaneous and informal, but always starting off with praising the Lord. It is a quiet petition that God touch this person, that he heal the specific illness. I usually ask also that the medication have the right effect and not have any bad side-effects. It's not a lengthy sort of thing. I wish in some ways it could be more, but in the context of my practice, and in the limited amount of time I can allot per patient, I can't get involved in any long-drawn-out prayer.

The ideal situation would be to be able to spend more time with each patient. I am not saying that I would like to do that, but it would be more in line with what I see around me in terms of our relationship with God, and in terms of praying with people. I know that I have been changing over the eleven years of my practice. I don't let myself get up-tight and over-rushed the way I did in the early years. I think things are fairly stable around here. Some aspects aren't as good as I would like them to be, and other things are even better. I'm getting more personal satisfaction out of my work, and I have a feeling that the patients now are more satisfied than they used to be.

I can almost put my hand on the reason for improvement and change in my practice of medicine and surgery. It's been the result of my involvement in the charismatic renewal—my wife and I—for about ten years. I suspect that most physicians would not consider prayer as part of their professional expertise or integral to their medical practice the way I do. Some of the surgical operations I do, like head and neck cancer work, and ear surgery, are more critical than ordinary medicine. I also do tonsils, adenoids, and facial plastic surgery. I take this work seriously and I pray silently before every procedure. Occasionally there will be a patient who asks me to pray with him or her in the operation room and, of course, I am glad to do that. But most of the time when they get that close to the operation they are already somewhat sedated and are not always aware of wanting to pray.

Do you ever see the kind of thing that Frank MacNutt, Oral Roberts and Barbara Schleman talk about: physical healing through prayer?

Several things have happened. Sometimes people get well unexpectedly, but let me back up a little. I believe it is incumbent on me to use my medical knowledge as best I can, and I use the prayer dimension also in the appropriate situation. Now there are people I pray for and they don't know it. I have prayed silently for a couple of people with sudden hearing loss—and they got better very quickly. I had other recent occasions of that. With one particular patient I said, "Let me tell you what I did while I was treating you." I wanted her to go to the hospital, but she couldn't because she was taking care of her elderly mother. So I sort of asked the Lord just to look over the situation and make up for the lack of my medical treatment because I couldn't put her in the hospital, and in two days she was remarkably better. I told her about it afterwards and it seemed to build her faith. Some people get well in the regular routine fashion; others seem to get well a bit faster than you expect, and then other people don't get better at all, or complications will set in. So I see the whole gamut of situations.

All the physician can do, or any other health care person, is to arrange the best conditions under which a cure can normally take place. Some doctors I know just say, "I leave the rest up to God." When I first got involved in the renewal I used to do a lot of estimating and evaluating in terms of what God has healed in the patient and what I have healed. After I read Sirach 38 often enough I realized that there is no such dichotomy. Everything about us is in God's dominion. So I don't much concern myself with whom did God heal and whom did I heal. If the patient gets well that's all I'm honestly interested in, regardless who gets credit. I know there are people who talk about percentages of cures at large healing services. Didn't you have some specific percentage breakdowns in your book on the charismatic movement?

Yes, but the figures came from the members, not from medical doctors who, I suspect, don't attribute their success to God.

That's probably the norm because the primary interest and intention the doctor has is in getting the patient well. He makes his choice of treatment and does the medical things he finds acceptable, whatever has the best chance of getting the person better, whether it's an operation or a medical treatment regimen. I think we can say in all reverence that even the deeply religious doctor is not going to substitute a prayer for a known medical formula. In most ways I don't think I'm very different from other medical professionals, at least in the essential thrust of medicine and surgery. It's true that some people come here to my office because they know I believe in prayer and am willing to pray with them. Now, I don't advertise that. The last thing I need is to have a crowd of people stacking up at the front door looking for faith healing.

The medical profession has become so technical and rational and precise that there isn't any room for spirituality.

I guess that's because you can't define or measure or evaluate prayer and the grace of God. When I was in medical school and in residency training the total thrust was the acquisition of scientific knowledge and its application. The thing you were respected for was your ability to make a diagnosis and to prescribe treatment, and whether or not you had any spirituality was irrelevant.

Probably it is still that way today in medical training, but since the publicity about Kübler-Ross' book, I think more folks are aware of the need to minister to people who are dying. I know that I have changed my own attitudes. If I have a patient who is going to die I think I should discuss that fact with the patient. I think patients have a right to know what is happening, and I usually encourage them to put their house in order, not from a financial point of view, but I always ask them, "Where do you stand with God?"

I had one situation that really helped build my faith. This man had cancer of the tongue and there was not a lot I could do save for cobalt radiation. It dragged on for nine months, and when it was obvious that he was heading for the end I asked him the question about being straight with God. He said, "Doc, I'm an old sea captain. I was at sea for forty years. I used to be a Catholic, but you know I haven't been to church." I figured out what parish he was in and I asked the pastor to go to see him. The guy went to confession and I really regard that I did more for him that way than anything medically that I ever did. I got a call on a Saturday afternoon from the man's family who said he was in severe pain. I went over to see him and stayed to pray with him. The family told me later that he then calmed down, had rested, wasn't uncomfortable anymore, and went out very peacefully and quietly. I don't want to say that that should be a normal procedure, but that is the kind of thing I have seen happen in my practice.

Physicians tell me that many people are sick because they are not at peace with themselves. Does that sound reasonable?

They have emotional problems that bring on headaches and neckaches. These are the people who usually want a sedative or a tranquilizer, but most of the time I don't prescribe it for them. I had a couple in here a few months ago, and the lady had a bunch of symptoms that didn't add up physically. I asked her if she was having any kinds of problems in her life. She really unloaded right there in front of her husband. She ventilated the thing that had been eating at her for the past six months. It was that her husband had insisted on moving to a part of the city where she knew no one and didn't like it at all. I don't know if and when they resolved that, but she certainly did not need medical attention.

Do you sometimes feel that you are doing the work of the clergy?

Not really, but I cooperate with them all the time. I am not taking the place of a priest or minister, but if I see people with a serious problem or who look as though they need to talk I encourage them to contact their pastor. I had a very serious cancer case, a man from out in the country. I met his minister who was a Baptist preacher, and we discussed the situation. I operated on him twice, but the second time I realized he was in real trouble and there was not a lot more I could do. I shooed his wife and son out of the room and had a serious talk with him about putting his house in order. When he went home he saw his minister regularly, and died three or four months later. He was a man of good solid faith in God.

Now that man was ready to die and I didn't expect anything else. Death is an experience everybody must have, and anyone who thinks he can escape it is pretty silly. But I do ask myself time and time again, "Why didn't so-and-so get better?" There are cases you expect to be healed and they aren't. It seems to me that we pray mainly for healing, and there's no good answer when it doesn't happen. As Christians, we have the obligation to pray for people. I think that is what God intends us to do. Of course, as a physician, I do the best I can medically. That's also what God wants me to do. In terms of other consolations of religion, I recall that as children we were taught to offer up our suffering to share in the passion of Jesus.

It is a basic Christian mystery that redemption comes through suffering, but I confess I find it difficult to locate positive value in pain and suffering. I believe that God's general will is that a sick person be healed in any given situation. I realize that we all have to have a fatal illness, and my approach would not be to reverse that fact. I could not say to a patient, "Let's see first if this is going to be a fatal illness for you. If it does not look that way we will pray for your healing." To me that would not be an appropriate approach. On the other hand it would not be terribly constructive of me simply to advise the sick person to "offer it up." I would then be out of business pretty soon because all the people who come in here are looking to get well. There may be a fair number of believers who have a concept of redemptive suffering, but even they, when they walk into this office, want to get well.

They are not really interested in philosophizing about whether or not their pain and illness can be a positive experience.

Are you and I simply the products of a comfort-loving painless culture? When was the last time you heard a sermon that we should mortify ourselves, fast and do penance?

I have heard that quite recently but not in the context of medical practice or even in my parish church. People who are members of the charismatic covenant community do talk about fasting and about doing penance. We do have a religious motivation, but I am not sure how much these modern so-called penances hurt anybody. Take somebody like myself who likes to eat. When I gave up eating between meals during Lent that wasn't fun at all, but we would hardly call it suffering.

The old rules about fast and abstinence have been greatly modified by the church, and it looks as though most of the hunger in the world is involuntary. Millions of people who are starving in the third world, and even here in America, are certainly not asking for suffering. There's a difference between someone who seeks suffering for the sake of Christ and identifying with the cross compared to someone who is innocently on the way to work today, gets hit by a car, and now has two broken legs. I am not sure you can equate the saints who inflicted pain on themselves with people who are homeless and hungry now through no fault of their own. They may or may not know what has caused their pain, but they know it was not their fault.

I'm sure they also wonder why they are the victims and not some other people. Sometimes we don't know the cause of pain. If a man has a hangover from drinking too much last night he knows the cause of his headache. The man in the auto accident knows what caused his pain, but there are people in sick beds who have no explanation, and they are often the patients who bring up the question of sin and sickness. "What did I do wrong that this happened to me?" Every doctor has to deal with these guilt feelings. I remind them of the story from the scriptures about the blind young man and the Pharisee who asked Jesus, "What did he do wrong to merit this?" Jesus said he didn't do anything wrong and neither did his parents. I try to negate their feelings of guilt and point them in a different direction. In the long run, I would have to say that why people suffer is a mystery.

But the patient persists, "That's right, Doc. I'm not guilty, but why do I have to suffer?"

That is the crunch that calls for faith. If you believe that there is a God who has an orderly plan and providence for humanity, probably that's the only way it makes sense. If there is no God, then it doesn't make any sense, and there is no value to anyone's suffering. Then, again, there is no value to life either. There is also a lot about medical practice that remains mysterious and unexplained.

Let me give you an interesting and puzzling paradox. A lady in her late forties came to me six years ago with cancer of the tonsil, and she had a lymph node which was indicative of spread. I gave her cobalt radiation and did a jaw and neck section on her, a head and neck cancer operative procedure. She is now more than five years post-treatment, and her chances statistically should be one in four to be still alive at this time. For all practical purposes that lady is cured of head and neck cancer, and that of course is a great joy.

But the thing about her that I have never understood is how come she also has so many other problems. She has hepatitis. She is not a drinker, but she has cirrhosis of the liver. She has had different other medical ailments that really dragged her down from time to time, and yet when it comes to the crunch, the big cancer thing, she has done rather well. She comes up with one illness after another, but she has tolerated them. She has had her down moments, but generally she has become a witness to other people. We have prayed together and shared the Lord, and she has become a real evangelist of sorts. I am not sure I could be anywhere as strong as she is under the circumstances.

Her secret, if I can make a good guess, is that she is close to God. I think that the religious influence a person like that can exert on other people, fellow sufferers as well as professional medical people, emerges from her own religious experience. That has to be true too for the nurse and the doctor who can bring the spiritual qualities of their expertise into the sick room. Each of them, I think, has somehow encountered God.

You mean that you have to have a conversion experience yourself?

I'm talking about the health care persons who succeed in ministering spiritually to sick people. Their ability to bring the consolations of religion to the person who is suffering depends in large measure on their own religious experience, whether they have met God, whether they have a strong faith. It seems to me that while it is God who does the healing it is the individual health care person who has to have some spiritual readiness. I know that there are groups of medical people like those in the Holistic Association, and maybe their preparedness is collective. Periodically I get communications from the Christian Medical Foundation in Tampa, but I don't know much about them. Maybe there is a whole group who think alike and are able to do spiritual ministry on an organized basis. Here in this city it strictly depends on the individual person who is dealing with the individual sick patient.

There doesn't seem to be any basic training for this either in the medical profession or the schools of nursing, even though we keep hearing more and more about holistic health care.

Certainly things have been changing over recent years. More people are getting interested in religion even in the medical profession. The curriculum in medical schools is not opening up for courses in spiritual healing, but there is now a Christian Student Medical Club where I took my training. I attended a luncheon seminar they put on last spring, and they actually talked about the role of God in medical practice. One of the speakers was from the charismatic renewal, and he explained very clearly some of the topics we have been talking about here today. He was able to give instances of cures in which he was personally involved.

I'll say this too: There is regularly a section of the program called the "Chaplains' Corner" at the annual meetings of the American College of Surgeons. The last time I attended, two years ago, there were about fifty people there listening to speeches by a general surgeon and two hospital chaplains. The clergymen were involved with the problems and the training of chaplains, but the surgeon had some interesting things to say. The thrust of his talk was that when you take the history of a patient you should also include what he called the spiritual history. This helped to know better how to deal with the patient's reaction to pain and to the seriousness of the illness.

I wonder what the content of a spiritual history would be. It should certainly not be a confession.

No, it's just a parallel to your medical history. The kind of questions I often ask seriously sick persons: Do you believe in God? Does he have a place in your life? What do you think God wants from you while you are in pain and suffering? We do a spiritual history of this kind when we meditate about God's healing power in our charismatic prayer meetings. It unfolds our personal relation with God.

VI

You Cry with Patients

Nurse Dolores is a Catholic R.N.
working on the hematology and cancer units of a large private research
hospital

Did your training as a nurse prepare you to deal with the spiritual dimensions of health care?

I attended a nursing school attached to a Catholic hospital run by the Daughters of Charity. At a Catholic college close by I took the further academic courses leading to the bachelor of science degree, and I have been a registered nurse now for the past six years. We had the advantage of a solid education in Catholic philosophy and theology. Practically all the girls there were Catholics; they lived together and really pushed the importance of religion. The sisters and the faculty did not encourage us to make converts or to put our religious values on the patients. We had priests and ministers and rabbis lecture to us about death and dying and what we should do in the event. They said that if the patient wanted to pray we could pray also if we felt that we could do that. Otherwise, we should get someone else to come in and pray with the patient.

Are most of your patients seriously ill?

I think you could say that. I'm in the hematology unit where they have all kinds of blood disorders, leukemia, hemophilia, cancer. Most of my patients are early middle-aged, and that could be discouraging because they are so young. We also get a lot of endocrine patients, like diabetics, but they don't seem to be as bad as the others.

Do you ever get discouraged or depressed?

Not really, at least not anymore. After a while I got used to this kind of work and I like it a lot. The only way to do it is to get really involved with your patients. For example, we have one man on the unit who is forty-five and had leukemia diagnosed ten months ago and is now in serious condition. Another nurse and I took his wife out to lunch and talked with her about her feelings, about the diagnosis of leukemia, and how her husband is dealing with it. We just asked her one day if she would like to get away from the hospital for a while. That meant a great deal to her. She is brave and was willing to talk about death and what changes that would make in her life. We got to be really good friends with this woman because we were with her husband every day. You don't hide the facts from these patients. If they spike a fever they have to know about it because it's important for them; it may be the difference of whether or not they can go home.

How do you see spirituality in the work you are doing?

Well, if I had my way I would like to see the spiritual aspect more out in the open. We have to be careful in a secular place like this. You just can't come right out and approach people about God. The patient might not take it the right way. Even back in the Catholic hospital where I trained I would have loved to pray with all my patients, but I always had to kind of feel my way through it and see whether or not they would be open to that. While it was predominantly Catholic there was always a certain percentage of Protestant patients, and a lot of these were elderly people. If a little old lady had a Bible next to her bed, I'd know that she would really appreciate it if somebody would sit down and offer to pray with her. They would all love to say the Lord's Prayer, or read the twenty-third psalm, "The Lord is my shepherd." There are these old black ladies who were very dedicated to their religion. That would just make their day, even more than the pill you give them for their arthritis. It was very touching. They would start to cry and would say, "Thank you very much for praying with me."

In the eyes of this hospital's administration I may be doing more than a nurse is required to do, but I say it's a significant aspect of nursing. The human contact with the patients includes the sharing of something so precious to them like God, religion and the Bible. It may mean more to the patient than a technical nurse coming in and saying, "It's time to take your medicine," or even more than the chaplain coming in and saying, "If there's anything I can do for you, let me know. The Lord bless you. I'll see you later." Then he walks out without a word about God or prayer or church or religion.

You obviously feel there is a spiritual dimension to nursing, besides the physical and psychological.

Oh yes, I believe they all go together. It's all part of the one person. I mentioned the effect it had on the persons I prayed with and recited the psalms. I wish I could feel free to include that all the time, and just regularly say to every patient: "Would you like me to pray with you?" But you have to be careful in this hospital because it's kind of as though you're over-stepping yourself. The best you can do is watch for an opening. You might see someone with a rosary, and that's a good way to open up a conversation. You can remark, "That's a very pretty rosary," or you tell them, "My rosary isn't as nice as yours." So, they know where you are coming from as a Catholic. Sometimes a patient who is discouraged will say, "Well, I guess I'm just going to have to put this in God's hands." Nothing can be clearer than that, and I think it's silly that you have to take it very, very slowly. It's a very delicate situation. Why is it that way?

Americans seem to think that religion is very private and personal.

I think they look on religion like psychiatry. For instance, I could go to a patient's room and say, "The doctor has put in a consult for you to see the urologist." That's taken as normal procedure, but you can never walk in a patient's room and as easily say, "The doctor has put in a consult for you to see the psychiatrist." I was really almost afraid to tell that to patients because there is still a kind of stigma attached to mental illness, or even the suggestion that you have a psychiatric or a psychological problem. You have to be very careful; otherwise the patient complains to the doctor himself, "This nurse told me you want the shrink to come to see me. What are you talking about? I don't need any psychiatrist." It's almost like that with religion. You may try to bring it to people, but the patient might object and say something to the doctor. It's a funny thing about religion, and maybe the reluctance isn't as great as most nurses imagine it to be. I guess there are a lot of nurses who are just secular and not concerned about a patient's religion.

Was anything like this mentioned in the orientation sessions when you first came to work here?

They did have an orientation program for a week of generalized things such as how to get a parking permit and where to park your car, and the time and place of meals. There were a lot of ordinary routine items like that. Then I went to the nursing division where they gave me a few days on orientation and then put me to work. I thought the orientation could have included something like psychological counseling, or some instruction to call a clergyman when a patient is near the end, but there was nothing like that. We don't have a head chaplain or organized pastoral care department or anything of the sort. The only way I knew there is a chapel was I saw a sign somewhere with an arrow pointing "To Chapel." I asked one of the nurses where it was. She said, "I think it's on the second floor but it doesn't seem to be open now. I think they are redoing it." This is a non-denominational hospital, but they allow all different kinds of ministers to come in. When I first got here one of the ministers made a point of introducing himself to me. He may have been a layman from one of the Protestant churches. I know he wasn't a Catholic. He said, "I just wanted to let you know if you ever need anything, or if you have a patient who wants spiritual guidance, please contact me." I was impressed by that, but I never saw him again. Religion does not seem to be of any official importance around this hospital.

In a way that's a disappointment, but I've gotten used to it. When I first got out of nursing school one of my biggest things was that I wanted to work in a Catholic hospital, but I couldn't find an opening and I thought I'd come here for the time being because this is one of the better hospitals as far as medical care is concerned. That would give me a lot of chances to really learn, and some things I didn't want to learn. For instance, early on I had a patient who went for an abortion and that really upset me. They don't do abortions here unless it's medically therapeutic, as they call it. I had never taken care of a patient who had had an abortion. It came as a shock to me. That was something I had to deal with, and at the time I really didn't know how to deal with it. I didn't meet any of her relatives, but I suspect that in her case, and in later instances, the family didn't know about it.

You did give me one example of dealing with a relative. Can you tell me other examples?

Yes, I had a very beautiful experience just a week before I graduated from nursing school. I was on the cancer ward and had a patient who was dying, and it was just a matter of days. The family asked us nurses to come into the room. I guess they had it clearly anticipated. As a nurse you do a few things that you can, like taking the blood pressure, but you know that doesn't make any difference. The Baptist minister was there, and all the family: the wife and children, the children's husbands and wives, and their children. There was myself and two other nurses, and we all stood around and held hands and we prayed as he took his last breath and died.

The minister prayed spontaneously. He thanked the Lord for this man's life on earth, the fruits of his life and labor, and thanked God for his beautiful wife and his beautiful children, and that the acceptance of his death was just the continuation of life in eternity. Of course, the children were crying, but it was a peaceful type of crying. They were saying, "Take him home, Jesus. We know you have him, Jesus." It was very touching, and we cried with the family. It was very beautiful because I was able to express my feelings just the way I felt about this man openly and in front of these other people. I always still feel that way about my patients now. There are many patients that I feel very close to, so that when they die I myself cry with the family. I do not feel ashamed of doing that, and I don't think it's unprofessional to do that.

The family and relatives are not always so emotional. Sometimes they are very matter-of-fact. One of my patients was dying, and the doctors had told the husband she would be going soon. He couldn't get here till three o'clock in the morning, and the first thing he asked was, "How will I know when she is dead? Will she just stop breathing and will I know what to do?" I had never had a patient's relative come to me with a question like that. He may have been grieving, but he didn't show it. I said to him, "Your wife is comfortable. She's got the morphine drip going, so she's not feeling any pain. You are the one who has to go through this." We offered him a cup of coffee which he took, and he just sat there smoking and waiting. I have no doubt that he loved his wife very much.

What else can you tell me that I haven't asked you?

Only this. All of these things are great that you want to do for a patient and the family: their psychological needs, their physical needs, their spiritual needs. I'm an idealistic person. Maybe too much so. I think of all these things and I want to do them just right, but when you have eighteen patients on the unit, and five or six of them are close to death, and you are the only nurse, it's not realistic. Sometimes it's almost frightening to me because there are so many needs and you can't meet them all. As a matter of fact, you can't begin to touch even half of these needs.

I think this is a problem in this part of the country where the hospitals have a real shortage of nurses. It's really not as bad here in this hospital as it is in some hospitals, but I'm on this wing with all these patients, just me and one aide. She is doing the care, like making the beds and giving baths, and I'm responsible for all the treatment and the medication. You have to deal with problems like X-ray calls and what tests can and can't be scheduled today. In the meantime, some of your patients on the hall are dying. You could spend all day just in one room with that patient and the family members trying to comfort them. You can't do it, and sometimes you become so frustrated, and discouraged, and depressed, and so you feel empty.

Were you prepared for this kind of thing in nursing school?

Yes, but it was in a kind of abstract way that couldn't really express it or define it. After a while you learn how to face reality and it kind of hardens you. I think it's still doing that to me. As a nursing student I was so idealistic and I guess I had to go through this reality shock eventually. It's normal to change through experience, and you've got to accept the fact that you can't do it the way you did it in school. When I was in training I was responsible for only two patients. Imagine that!

I admire some of the older nurses who still have the human touch. Our supervisor here has been at it for over twenty-five years and she is a marvelous person. She doesn't have much patient contact, but I happened to see her with a patient who was dying of cancer and just the way she talked with the woman and her family. She expressed concern in her voice which was soft and had a soothing effect on everybody in the room. She gently put a catheter in the woman so she wouldn't have to worry about anything. She was on morphine drip and that means the end. What was important was the way she did it. She went in there and did the technical job she had to do, but in such a way that this was not more important than the dying patient and her family. What I'm saying is very intangible, very difficult to describe. It's an attitude. It's a tone of voice. It's compassion, or whatever, and I think it's an expression of religion, of Christian love.

This supervisor certainly was not hardened by her experience.

That's right. When I say you get hardened I don't mean that the type of care you give gets less gentle. I mean you can't be idealistic in a non-idealistic setting when you can't always do everything you'd like to do for people. I suppose that's what I meant to say. Let me say that sometimes I want the patients to die. They are suffering and miserable and in so much agony that I will actually pray, "God, don't let this patient linger." I will pray for the family, even though it hurts them that the person is gone. I will say, "Thank you, God, that this patient is not suffering anymore." I'm not saying that God makes us suffer, but I'm thanking God for bringing relief.

Do you see sick people who are afraid to die?

Sometimes there is fear but it's usually not in the last stages of dying, and it's a bad experience for the family more than for the patient. You get some family members who just don't want to accept the fact of death. They say, "Oh, she is going to get better." They will go out and spend money on sandwiches and salads and big chocolate malts to try to get them to eat when the patient can hardly breathe. They figure if they could just get her to eat she would get better. You know, it's their way of coping. You can't take away their hope, but what can you do? I just try to support the family and make them feel they are part of the care. For example, if I have medication to give I ask, "Do you think she would rather have it mixed with Seven-Up or with fruit juice?" That way they feel part of what's going on. I ask them, "Do you want to give her the medicine, because she seems to respond better when you are giving it to her?"

But there's another kind of situation when the patient seems quite willing to die. One of the things that the nurse sees is the large number of people who die peacefully and just sort of slip away. You have to remember that's the effect of modern medication which is doled out gradually. They start with a mild pain relief like Tylenol Codeine, that's Tylenol Number Three. Then they'll move them to Deloric which is a fairly strong narcotic, and then to methadone. Finally, they get the so-called morphine drip. Then you know the doctor has given up on the patient.

But the doctor is not as close to the sick person as the nurse.

And some of them don't really care. I was talking with an intern the other day who told me that a certain lady had just died. It was unexpected to me and I told him it was really a shock. He said, "You nurses ought to get used to this. You all are with them more than we are." Since I work on the shift I do, we get a lot of the interns and younger doctors. I had a cancer patient who was only twenty-five, and I told this doctor what a hard time I was having with that. He said, "Well, there's nothing I can do for her. She's going to die. I can't help that." He totally blocked it out. He doesn't deal with it at all because he is just rotating through this service for a few months. If somebody dies of cancer he couldn't care less about it. He just doesn't want anything to do with it.

It is a cover-up for his emotions, I think, but he's too proud and independent, and he really needs to talk about it. He's only about twenty-five, and that's young for a doctor. It's going to cause a lot of problems with him later on. A lot of doctors think they are God; at least they want to be like God. They feel that they shouldn't fail. I don't think that when a patient dies it is necessarily a failure. To me, of course, dying is not the end of everything. It's more a crisis for the family than it is for the patient—although if someone told me I was going to die right now, that would probably be more than I could handle. But it would be harder on my family, I think, than on me.

One thing I think is that doctors and nurses need to get together, especially since as nurses we work closer with the patients than they do. We really need to talk it out, to share our experiences and to share our feelings. No matter what you think you can do, you're going to have a touch of despair when a patient doesn't respond and doesn't get better. There's bound to be discouragement, especially for doctors. They don't like to fail, and we don't either, but they've got to know that we care about the patients too. The doctors don't really communicate effectively to know that we are there for the same reasons they are. Ultimately everything we do is for the patient, not for ourselves. I've had the impression over the years that doctors don't realize it hurts us to fail as much as it hurts them, and it hurts them as much as it hurts us. We are totally in this together, and we need each other.

VII

Spiritual Health in the Navy

Chaplain Frederick is a navy officer assigned to the pastoral care department of a large navy hospital

You're a priest wearing a navy officer's uniform. Do you have any special training for hospital chaplaincy?

Every branch of the military service has a detailed job description for every possible assignment. This is true also of chaplains within the navy, and working in a hospital is only one of the many positions we may be called on to fill. So, we have a *Handbook for Navy Chaplains*, produced by a number of chaplains experienced in ministry to sick personnel, and describing in great detail the job expectations and characteristics of pastoral health care.

As you might expect, the modern U.S. navy goes far beyond the approved *Handbook* in preparing chaplains for hospital service. I took the four units of the Clinical Pastoral Education program at one of our Veterans' Administration hospitals and then did a full year of pastoral residency in the psychiatric department of the navy hospital. In all this formal training there was no input at all about the pastoral dimension, how I could function specifically as a priest, and what was my unique religious contribution to the patient, that would not be made by a doctor, a nurse, a medical corpsman. There was a strong emphasis on dealing with your own feelings in relation to sick people, their families and all the hospital personnel. The training was geared almost exclusively to psychology and counseling.

What are the reasons why the program is so limited?

Some of the CPE supervisors thought that priest chaplains are tempted to breeze through the sacramental ministration and never get to know the sick person. And maybe there was something to that in the old stereotype of hospital chaplains. He goes into the room, introduces himself by saying, "I'll bring you Communion and have the anointing while you're here," and that's it. In the old days, if you didn't have this bag of tricks, as it were, to bring with you, what would you do? But I've got to say that more than one Protestant minister has said that in many ways they envy the priests who have a definite procedure to follow in the sick room. They have no conventional formula of that kind and are thrown back on their own resources.

The other thing the supervisors said—and I tend to agree with this—it can be very uncomfortable being in the presence of someone who is ill. You can start avoiding a lot of things, and you can start talking just piously, never really dealing with anything that the patient wants to say. My own case is an example of this. My mother died very suddenly and very unexpectedly. I had two weeks off after the funeral. When I went back to the hospital and was making the rounds I came to a room where the patient was very similar to my mother in looks. I could only stay in that room for five minutes. I mean, I had to get out. Every day then I avoided going into that room. I talked to the supervisor about that. I was dealing with my grief that affected my seeing that woman who physically reminded me of her.

What is your hospital day like?

The first thing to know is that we are not limited just to navy personnel, but we take care of people both active and retired, and their dependents. So, it's like any general hospital in the city that has every department from gynecology to geriatrics. The normal daily in-patient census here is between 450 and 500, and we have five navy chaplains, three Protestants and two Catholics. I don't think there's a navy formula for the ratio of chaplains to patients, but it seems to be one for every fifty patients. The total staff to operate this hospital is close to a thousand people.

I guess by temperament my approach to patients has to be low key. On a normal day I spend a lot of time on the wards, and just kind of stroll around. First, I stop at the nursing station because they are the ones who have most contact with the patients. They tell me who is having problems, and they know pretty well who might be helped by a visit from the chaplain. I then visit the patient, and if it is the first time I identify myself as the Catholic priest and tell them I'll be glad to come to visit with them, and that the sacraments are available if they want them. I usually put the responsibility on them for requesting that, but the Catholics see me every day. We have a large cancer ward with a lot of dying people, and I spend a great deal of time with the terminally ill.

I remember one cancer patient who survived a year after she was diagnosed as having leukemia. I'd see her every day, and some days she would be very, very depressed and needed somebody to cry with. Or there would be days when she would have what she called theological problems. She was a woman who didn't have a strong faith initially, but when she got sick she realized that her life was coming to an end. She was very concerned about her four young children, and I would sit there and help her compose letters to them. She began to question herself and her relationship with God. I remember coming back from vacation and talking with her for more than an hour. When I came out of the room the nurses said, "How come she's laughing so much now after she has been so depressed?" I said, "Maybe you all treat her as though she is already dead. She's still alive and very interested in everything." I don't think I ever went in with anything definite and clear to say. It would be whatever the patient wanted it to be.

A lot of times in the navy hospital you meet patients who had fallen away from the church and have no interest whatsoever in coming back to the church. Of course I keep visiting them, and in a couple of cases I think that's what turned them around. But it happens very infrequently that they come back to the faith. They have no interest in the church. They still have their own kind of faith in God which doesn't necessarily have a doctrinal dimension that is Catholic. They do have a relationship to God, and we would pray together.

I remember one Sunday being called by a woman who said, "You've got to come over right now and anoint my brother. He's dying." I told her, "Well, I've seen your brother every day for four months and he has never said he is a Catholic." At the foot of his bed there was this card with N.P. on it, "no preference" of religion. So, I came over and chatted with him and he said, "Oh, Father, I was baptized a Catholic, but I gave it up a long time ago. I've no interest in that side of religion. I believe in God in my own way, and I trust him." Anyway, we said some prayers together and I let it go at that. When I came out of the room his sister was in an uproar because I didn't anoint him. I said, "What's going on here? Your brother made it very clear that the sacraments have no meaning for him." It turned out that she herself was away from the church for a long, long time and his dying just stirred up all kinds of thoughts in her. So we sat down and had a long conversation. It was much more her need than it was her brother's need.

That man was very placid. Have you had patients who are angry at you, or angry at God?

Yes, both. For example, we had a little boy dying in pediatrics of what is called the "prune syndrome," where the child is literally shriveling, and it's awful. This young mother came every day to be with the child, and when I walked in I would get instant hostility from her. I'd try to talk with her and get curt answers. Well, I accepted that and just kept coming back. She had a second child who was having a difficult time dealing with his brother's dying. So one day she went to the charge nurse and asked if she had something to read about dying. The nurse said, "Why don't you go to see the chaplain? He has some knowledge in this; maybe he can give you some suggestions or something to read."

Well, she walked into my office and said, "I'm just going to take two minutes of your time. I want you to give me something to read about dying." I invited her to sit down and relax. Then all the anger and hostility came spurting out, blaming God, and why is God doing this to her. I just sat there and let her talk for two hours without interrupting her, and I didn't engage her in combat. She was angry and she was hurting, and she needed to say so. After she tired out and calmed down she herself said, "I really don't believe all this, that God is at fault. I don't know who to blame." Part of it was—as in many situations when a young child is dying—that it put a tremendous stress on the marriage. Her husband is a navy pilot and he put the ultimatum to her when he said, "As far as I'm concerned, Johnny died two years ago." She was so worried about the dying child, and so threatened by the loss of her husband, and really she was just over-whelmed. A lot of guilt came into it also because she had not been a practicing Catholic. She had fallen away from the church in her college years. After we had a number of talks she made up her mind to start going back to Church.

You just seem to let people ventilate. What's your answer when they say, "Why does God do this to me?"

I don't think that you have to answer that, because there really isn't any answer to it. I don't think that's what they are asking. They are terribly angry and frustrated, and they can't make any sense of their pain and suffering. Often they feel that there was something they didn't do right in the past, or that they neglected. They feel guilty, but rather than accept that they've got to put the blame out there somewhere. Sometimes they think God is punishing them, but I'm not sure I've met any people who really believe that. And I don't know how to answer that either. When that has come up many times I just stay quiet. I think ultimately it is a mystery, and I don't know what to say.

Perhaps you don't have to be a chaplain and wear a cross on your uniform to listen to angry people, but I see it as a function of the priest in the hospital. Medicine gives answers with narcotics but tries also desperately to avoid the ultimate questions. This is where the clergyman brings that dimension of hope, which is what Christianity preaches and is supposed to be all about, that God is gracious, that God is good. What I can give is not a narcotic like Valium. You're still going to hurt and suffer and feel pain. The chaplain, by his title and definition, represents an awful lot to the patients, and I am not saying that nobody else can do it, because nurses and doctors sometimes do that.

Are physicians ever concerned about the spirituality of patients?

Yes, I can give you examples. In particular, a very competent young navy doctor actually offers to pray with his patients. He says, "Sometimes they get scared and ask me 'Am I that sick, Doc?' and I try to tell them you don't pray only when you're sick." Often the doctors in the hospital come by and tell me about patients who are "in a bad way. They really need you, and I can't do anything with them. Please go and visit them." When our chief oncologist first came on board he gathered all the chaplains together and said, "You know that a lot of my patients are going to die, so you and I have to work very closely together. I believe you have an important function to perform."

I spent a week with Dr. Kübler-Ross at her place in California. She is a very strong proponent of the role of the chaplain, and she insists that the pastoral role is very distinct from the medical role. You have to give a lot of time to sick people, even if it is nothing more than to sit with them—especially into the early hours of the morning, because for critically ill people that's when they are most alone and most in need of someone there. She said that in her imaginary hospital the chaplain would be on duty from ten at night to eight o'clock in the morning. He would get his sleep during the day.

Is all of the pastoral care done exclusively by navy personnel?

Oh no, we have six volunteer nuns who come as visitors to the ward, and who are very well received. One sister especially, who has leukemia, is very popular. She made a hit with one young sailor who was extremely bitter because he knew his leukemia was fatal. He found out that the sister was still functioning and teaching, and living within the bounds of her illness. He was a Protestant and she was a Catholic nun, and it just turned him around. In fact, one day after about three weeks of visiting, he said, "Sister, do you fish?" She said, "Yes, would you like to go fishing?" So the two of them went off to the pier and went fishing several times. It was just her quiet persistence and the example of her own obvious faith that brought him around. These young sisters were teaching five days a week, but they came in three afternoons a week and were very helpful in cheering up the patients. I also have two retired nuns from the local high school who spend most of their time here. They do fantastic things just moving around with the patients and bringing Communion.

I've had some of the most meaningful sacramental experiences of my life in this hospital work. I remember a man coming in one day and saying, "Well, Father, I was just told I'm going to die. It will be soon, and I want to go to confession." He had it all put together, reviewed his whole life in the sacrament of confession, was anointed and received Communion. He was in the hospital for more than a week and was utterly serene the whole time. I think that's the other side of our pastoral care that we sometimes forget: that the patient also ministers to the chaplain. We had a young naval officer die here of cancer. He became a convert to the church in the last few weeks of his life; he almost seemed to become transparent with the reality of grace. I would go to his room, not to give him any assistance but just to be there with him. I remember one day when I brought him Communion I was surprised to see two doctors kneeling there at his bedside. There was just an aura about this young man.

That seems a remarkable effect of spiritual ministration. I don't want to press you for miracles, but isn't this miraculous?

Well, I wouldn't say miracles in the sense of complete cures because none of these people survived. I think that the quality of their life—the last months of their lives—changed dramatically. Certainly that was the religious dimension, the sacramental ministration, and that had a spin-off effect on other people. I recall one retired air force nurse who died of cancer. I used to bring Communion to her every day. She had very strong faith. She had actually been in battle zones, treating the wounded and the dying. As a nurse she had been dealing with death all her professional life, so this was no novel big deal to her. I remember going into her room on a gloomy rainy day and feeling quite down, and I said, "Isn't this a terrible day?" She said, "No, I think it's a great day. Look at the interesting way the rain splashes on the window. You get the feeling that it's nice and clean." I just think her cheerful attitudes were a dimension of her faith in God and her contact with Christ in the sacraments.

You say you felt down on that rainy day. Do you sometimes feel down because you see so much pain and suffering?

Yes, I do at times. In some cases you feel helpless and you don't know what you can say to anybody. You can feel so badly too for the families of patients and for the tragedies of people's lives. I recall an old sailor dying who said, "I'm over seventy-five years old, but I have never really lived my life." I could see this terrible sense of regret that he had missed everything worthwhile. He had pursued all the wrong things. I just felt terrible the day I heard that. But there are days of real spiritual uplift. We have daily Mass in the hospital, and some days we would have a remarkable attendance of doctors, social workers, psychiatrists, corpsmen, and nurses. When the relatives of a dying patient are there at Mass the people would be very supportive of them. I find a

great deal of spirituality in the hospital, and that helps to
cheer you up.

You mention relatives. Are they part of your responsibility?

Oh yes, very much so. Most chaplains make a very conscious effort to visit a patient whose family and relatives are
there. You just introduce yourself and let them know you're
available. Also, always be sure to go by the intensive care unit
where the relatives are sitting. Unfortunately in this hospital
the intensive care unit doesn't have a private little area for the
family. They are out in the hallway sitting there in chairs with
all the traffic going back and forth. They are hurting but they
don't want to make a scene, and they're wondering what's
going on back of that door. They are allowed to go in only five
minutes each hour, and they too need to be cared for. The
nurses can't say much to them because they're rushing in and
out. The relatives feel that nobody's paying any attention to
them. The chaplain can do them a lot of good.

Of course, I should mention that our sister visitors spend
time with the relatives. The social workers can do it. I remember a fine Jewish social worker at Presbyterian Hospital. We
sent a sailor there because we couldn't take care of his needs.
His parents came in from Michigan. Their boy was dying, and
I would go over there every day. This marvelous social
worker over there cared for that family in the most generous
kind of way. She had a good sense of humor, knew about the
sacraments for Catholics, and gave moral support and
strength to everybody around her.

Do you have many women patients in a navy hospital?

Not, of course, as many as males. The women sailors
tend to be younger, except some of the veteran navy nurses.
Then there are the wives and other dependents of navy personnel. A woman patient may be involved and worried about
the so-called theological issues like abortion, or birth control,
or second marriage, or divorce. The abortion issue gets special attention by the psychiatrists who have to review each

case, and they respect the Catholic teaching. They call me each time and say, "There's a Catholic lady who's going to have an abortion." I would always go up to the ward, not to engage in combat, because by that time she had already made up her mind. I want her to know that the church is also in the business of reconciliation. Whatever forced her to this decision didn't have to keep her away from the church. In eight out of ten cases the woman would say, "Please come back." It is really no time to have an argument with her. It's been an agonizing decision to make, especially for a woman who is trying to live the faith, and has some commitment to the Church and to Christ. It's a lot different with the woman who couldn't care less about God and religion. She just says, "Oh, it's nice to see you. Thanks for coming by."

As a final question, is abortion just a routine procedure?

Maybe it is medically, but we have had a serious problem when many of the nurses and operating room technicians—not all Catholics—were refusing to be part of the abortion procedures. It created a tremendous tension among the staff in that department. They were being accused of sloughing off their jobs. We had several meetings with them, explaining what the Catholic teaching is, and why conscience could keep people from taking part in that. The military is itself very careful to respect the conscience of its personnel.

VIII

Student Nurses
and Pastoral Care

Sister Dorothea is the director of a
school of nursing affiliated with a 400-
bed Catholic general hospital

*What is the difference between a Catholic school of nursing and other
kinds of nursing schools?*

From a strictly medical, academic and technological perspective I don't know that you would find any essential and
notable difference. I am sure that most nursing schools today
are training the students to care for the total person. This is
the popular holistic approach to health care. Both would be
giving the same required academic courses and using the
same textbooks. We don't have any particularly Catholic textbooks. In our philosophy, maybe we would have an emphasis that another school might not have on the spiritual care of
the patient as truly deserving of dignity and respect. I would
hope that all nursing schools do the same thing.

Nevertheless, I like to think that we have something
going for us in our allegiance to Christianity. Jesus Christ led
the way for us and we are his followers. For myself personally, and in my profession, my beliefs have always been very
important. I entered a religious community to serve God, and
I am following a particular call. Maybe that's old-fashioned

language these days, but the fact that I am here makes a difference. I don't think I contradict myself when I say that a
Catholic hospital should make a difference simply because of
our faith dimension. Perhaps we are not always conscious of
that fact, but I would hope that it is our highest level of motivation.

The students come here as high school graduates, most
of them from the Catholic schools where we hope they had
pretty good religious instruction. When they come in as
freshmen we give them some orientation with four hours of
instruction in the spiritual care of patients. They won't get
any formal training along these lines. We have the chaplains
come over and talk to the students about their own spiritual
life and about the spiritual care of the patients. I don't know
what else we could do, unless we put in a course in sacra-
mentology or contemporary religious thought. That's what
we did at one time, but the students didn't show up for it.

We do offer the students the opportunity to go to Mass
every day at noon when the majority of them are free. Very
few show up for weekday Masses. We don't run retreats ourselves, but we post the local retreats that are available. We
have six special liturgies during the year, such as at the start
of the semester and at Thanksgiving. I get a group of the students to plan the liturgy each time, and some of them do that
very well. They are all invited and strongly encouraged to attend, but no one is forced to come to them.

How does all this differ from your own years in nursing school?

I took my training right here in this very school well before I became a sister; it was back in the days before Vatican
II. Most of my teachers were lay people, and we had a priest
teach us the religion courses. I remember when we readied
the patients for the anointing, we did much more of that. We
also prepared them for Communion. The student set up the
table at the head of the bed with the crucifix and two candles.
We were more involved in that kind of thing in those days,
but all that has changed. Now the sacrament is given by eucharistic ministers, like myself, without bell or candle, in a

much more informal way. I suppose there is not much difference in the basics you learn in freshman year, how to make the bed, feed and bathe the patient, before you get into more professional things. When they get to the last semester they are putting it all together. The students learn team nursing and leadership nursing and management. They are on a day and evening rotation and work together with the charge nurse in a charge position.

In some ways it's more difficult these days. The demands on nurses have increased considerably. Only four or five years ago you would have less than half the patients get intravenous infusions. Now most of the patients get some type of intravenous treatment when they come into the hospital. There are all kinds of tests now that the patients are going through. Some time ago we didn't have the cat scanner, or any of the nuclear type equipment that is now in use. It was just simple X-rays. But now every patient on the unit may be going for five or six tests. The nurse has to give all the intravenous infusions, and she has to make sure that either she or the ward clerk has the requisitions for all the medications. You have two nurses doing all the treatments and medications on the unit, and you're lucky if you have two more nurses to take care of the patients.

It seems to me that nursing has become a much more developed profession with the nurses doing things that the physicians used to do, and I'm not sure that's a good thing. It takes the nurse away from spending more time with the patient, and I don't know how else to get around it. In some hospitals you have medical techs to do some of it, doing physiotherapy and respiratory therapy, and in some places you have pharmacists who will come up and give out the drugs.

Do you have a student dormitory?

Yes, it's still called the nurses' home, and most of the student nurses live here, but they are free to live at home with their family and commute to the hospital every day. Life is very different from the time I was a youngster in training. We had Mass every morning and night prayers together in the chapel. We had Benediction twice a week. There was no smoking permitted, and only a few of the girls dared to smoke away from the building. If we went out on a date, or with some classmates, we had to check out and also check in no later than eleven o'clock. There is no question that the principles of moral living and the high vocation of nursing were closely linked with Catholic beliefs and practices.

Although the nurses' home is much more open than the dormitory was in our day, we like to feel that we have a good community spirit. In the past I suppose the spiritual dimension of health care was taken for granted. And maybe it is now, even if we don't spell it out. We were sure that nursing was a special kind of vocation in the service of God and humanity. Nowadays we call it a professional commitment, a personal concern emerging from the holistic philosophy. These youngsters in general do not appear to be as pious as we were, and they want more freedom to express themselves, but they are putting in the hours and exhibiting tender loving care that looks like the practice of Christianity to me.

Do they appreciate their professional training?

We have over two hundred student nurses enrolled in the three years, some of them on scholarship, most of them paying the modest tuition we require. The retention rate is pretty good, with a little more than ten percent dropout between freshman and senior year. They go through all their training in this hospital with the exception of psychiatry and pediatrics, which are provided at two other medical facilities. Through our tie-in with the Jesuit college they get thirty-four academic credits, and I'm working with the dean to try to get an upper-level division of nursing for R.N.'s. We'll see if we can get another thirty-four credits, and then the nurses can go out for two years more on a part-time basis and finish up with their bachelor degree.

I ought to say that we offer specialized training for nurses who may want it, not only our own nurses but some from other hospitals. Right now we are advertising for nurses for the course in hemo-dialysis. We are willing at this point to

train sixteen nurses in this specialty. There has been a turnover in dialysis nurses three or four times since we started
this course, and we are centrally the hemo-dialysis hospital
in this region. Younger people find the hours rather difficult,
so we are constantly educating people on our training program. It takes three months—one month in class work and
three months of clinical experience in the halls. We actually
do this training for four other hospitals. We do the same kind
of training courses in two other specialties: coronary care and
surgical care.

*Is there some area of nursing that the students find more difficult
than others?*

There are probably individual dislikes just as there are
individual preferences. All student nurses are routinely exposed to all aspects of nursing. Some don't like surgery and
the operating room; others find the intensive care unit a real
strain; some dislike their rotation in the emergency room.
These are the things they tell me, but for the most part they
learn to take them all in stride with some encouragement and
with more experience. If any one of these experiences—or all
of them—becomes intolerable for a particular student she
may drop out early in the course.

I have to say that they are not overfond of the night shift,
even when they have finished training, but they know they'll
be called on to do it. If there is one problem they all have in
their student years it is dealing with the relatives and families
of the patients. It's very hard to expect eighteen or nineteen
year old girls in training to go in and deal with the family.
They soon learn how to deal with the patient all right, but it's
much more difficult to deal with relatives and an anxious family. Nurses in general find that the hardest. We talk about it;
we teach it; but students tend to shy away from it even when
they have to do it.

When they are in their last semester they are on a day
and evening rotation, and it is in the evening shifts during the
visiting hours that they get a chance to see the families together. They know what is expected of them. Sometimes they

can learn more about their patients from talking with the family, at least, to understand the personality of the patient. In the normal course of a hospital stay, the family can usually see for themselves if the person is making much progress. You tell them the tests that are being planned, and give them whatever information is available. They feel more comfortable once they know what is being done and what efforts are being made.

But there are other family situations that the younger nurses and students can't cope with, and one of the more mature supervisors has to intervene. Patients are not the only ones who go through stages of denial. You often see the spouses or close relatives in great anxiety and unwilling to accept the diagnosis. They play the nurse against the doctor. They say, "The doctor told me a very different story. He didn't say the same thing that you are saying." It takes a great deal of maturity and a lot of realistic knowledge to recognize these contradictions. It may well be that the doctor was trying to soften the blow and giving the diagnosis in a more acceptable way than the nurse does. Families can be a lot of trouble for student nurses.

Do the doctors participate in training student nurses?

Except for some academic lectures delivered by members of the medical staff the doctors do not have any direct instructional role in the nurses' training and education. While they are on the wards they have the same professional relationship with the doctors that all the nursing staff has. It was the doctor who brought the sick person to the hospital and who has the ultimate responsibility for the treatment of the patient. Of course, the nurse is subordinate to the physician and is obliged to follow his directions in the care of the patient. On some few occasions the physician has complained about the incompetence of the trainee, but on other occasions older and more experienced nurses have complained about the arrogance of the doctor. Some of the doctors—and I think it is mainly the surgeons—are slow to admit that they are not always successful. They take it as a kind of personal defeat if the patient doesn't get well.

One of the questions brought up by bright young student nurses is whether their primary duty is to the patient or to the physician. They realize that the doctor has a great deal more medical knowledge than they will ever achieve, but they also know medical ethics and the *Code for Nurses* of the American Nurses' Association and the Florence Nightingale Pledge. The older nurse may sometimes have doubts about the efficacy of a medication ordered for the patient but will resist only from administering "harmful drugs."

There are only two common ethical problems that most nurses will even encounter. The first is the question of surgery for sterilization and even for abortion. These are absolutely forbidden in this Catholic hospital, so that neither nurses nor doctors have to make any moral decision about them.

The second problem is now with us and threatens to occur more frequently, and that's the dilemma of using extraordinary means to keep a patient alive. The machines are available to sustain life, or to resuscitate a dying patient, and are becoming more refined and efficient. Our philosophy here in the hospital is that the patient's doctor is not obliged to take the whole responsibility, or to make the decision by himself, to remove the life-sustaining apparatus. For example, in the case of an infant born with Down's Syndrome and duodenal atresia, a conference is called that includes the parents, the physician, one or more nurses, and always the head chaplain of the pastoral care department. More often the patient is an older person who has been through surgery and hospitalization and treatments to which he or she fails to respond.

Are the student nurses trained in pastoral counseling?

Here we get back again to the holistic notion of health care and say not only that the patient has spiritual needs as well as physical and psychological, but also that every person dealing with the patient is a whole personality: body, mind and spirit. I think we have a head start in Catholic health care because, in general, the people who get into this vocation have a basic desire to be of help to others; they have a concern and a compassion that you may not always find in other kinds of occupations. So, to answer your question, the student nurses are not expected to take the training units of clinical pastoral education, but they are taught to put into practice some of the psychological principles the CPE people always talk about. In other words, the bedside nurse is going to have a more personal relationship, and for a longer time, with the patient than the doctor or anybody else has.

The so-called spiritual foundations of nursing are implemented as soon as the student nurse begins the care of patients. That's on a daily basis when they are involved in making out the Communion lists for the priest to bring the sacrament. We've experimented with almost all hours of the day for the distribution of Communion, and we now have it scheduled in the afternoon from four to four-fifteen as the best time of the day. Nowadays, almost always, it is the sisters who are the eucharistic ministers. The young nurses, even the non-Catholics, are very respectful and say they like this practice. Another religious pattern we follow daily is five minutes of prayer at seven each morning over the public address system, by one of the sister visitors.

Are the chaplains on duty round the clock?

We have two priests in residence, and another who comes over to fill in for their days off. We have sister visitors, one on each floor, who are retired and experienced nurses themselves, and respond to calls even when they are off-duty. All of them serve as eucharistic ministers and are popular with both the patients and the nurses. We also have a large corps of lay people, mostly women, who regularly visit the sick. I'm not going to criticize our own people here. I think that with our resources we do as good a job as can be expected on what you call the spiritual dimensions of health care.

I think that in the future of health care in Catholic hospitals, pastoral care has to be the core department of the whole institution. It has to be a very dynamic department, giving leadership and courage and assistance to all other areas because they all have a role in the spiritual dimension. I want it to be recognized on the organizational chart as important as the laboratory, obstetrics, surgery, nursing, and I think it has to be seen as the hub around which everything else revolves. The director should be a woman, not necessarily a nun, who is also an expert supervisor of clinical pastoral education. You need a couple of Catholic chaplains, depending on your population, and some Protestant clergy, full-time or part-time. You need a definite group of trained volunteers who can be depended upon to make regular visits to patients. I don't think it's necessary that you have a priest in charge because sometimes a priest gets very involved in priestly things.

This is a very conservative area of the country. You have to make sure that the hospital administrators tie into this. Many administrators wonder why a hospital should pour money into a pastoral care department when they think they are able to get away with one chaplain. In the old days when we had a surplus of priests with little to do in the parish rectory, the hospital chaplain felt that he too could take three days off a week. And we often had old men who needed medical care themselves and couldn't be assigned to other kinds of work in the church.

Right now we have very few priests in this diocese who have been trained in CPE, and no Catholic hospital has a CPE supervisor and training program. There is beginning now in the diocesan seminary a series of six weekends of instruction, but that would be only part of their training. Right now, when priests are appointed by the bishop or by religious superiors, they go into hospital work without any specific health care training. We want young men and we want deacons—and it's time we get more young women—to get the Clinical Pastoral Education, and to receive a decent salary when they come into the hospital chaplaincy.

IX

Sacraments for Catholics

Father Sylvester is a Josephite priest,
director of the Catholic pastoral care
program at a 1,200-bed municipal
general hospital

Why do you take care of only Catholic patients?

For almost fifty years there was only one full-time chaplain in this hospital, a priest hired by the archbishop. At any given period there would be about 400 Catholic patients, more than enough to keep one priest busy. In 1966 the position opened up and my provincial asked me if I would like to take it. I live here in the hospital, in the same quarters shared by the resident medical staff and interns. It is a twenty-four hours a day job that takes all my energy just to administer the sacraments.

At what point did you start the pastoral training program?

It came out of a double kind of need in 1970 when I insisted on getting some help and when our seminarians needed the apostolic experience of so-called fieldwork in their course on pastoral theology. The program grew out of that. It was about that time also that I became a member of the National Association of Catholic Chaplains. I attended a two-week workshop for chaplains, and as a result of that I was certified as a hospital chaplain. That workshop was run under the auspices of the NACC, which is under the National Conference of Catholic Bishops. So it was not the Association for Clinical Pastoral Education. Of course, I had to get accreditation in order to have the training program approved, but it had its beginnings that way. And I had to be approved as supervisor of pastoral training, even though I do not hold rigidly to the four units of CPE.

Here the seminarians come to the hospital twice every week for a full year. I have approximately twenty-five at any one time. We are associated with a cluster of independent theological schools in this area, and I am the supervisor for their experimental apostolic ministry program, which now includes some sisters and some lay women. It is only in the last three years that we introduced a program for the training of deacons, and we encouraged their wives to participate as much as they can in the training of their husbands. So when the married deacons came to me for the clinical pastoral training the wives came along too. They couldn't very well just sit there idly in the lecture hall, so we assigned them a bevy of patients to take care of as well.

Tell me a little about the daily schedule.

They don't come into the hospital in the morning because of their academic program at the seminary. They come regularly at one o'clock for a lecture given by doctors and nurses, and some are given by me. Following the lecture they have their assignment of patients to visit for about two hours. That means they see the same patients in the same area week after week, or as long as the person is in the hospital. Of course, there is turnover of patients but the student stays pretty much in the same area or department for the whole year. After the patient visitation they come back to the conference room where we discuss the afternoon's experience on the ward. Usually I appoint a particular student to discuss the situation of one patient whose case is then probed by all the others. They usually finish that and go home at five o'clock.

As the program develops through the year, along about

the beginning of January their experience is expanded and each of them is required to spend eight hours as chaplain to the emergency room, on the four to midnight shift twice a month. Once they understand what is going on and have enough experience with the patients in the regular ward, we have two or three of the students working there in the emergency room at the same time. Their function is to meet the patients as they are brought in, be with them in the preliminary examination and help the physician as much as they can. This requires some understanding of what the doctor is doing and why. If it is a case of a patient being sutured they are there to lend a hand. The whole idea is that they are with the doctor and are part of the scene, and the patient is not alarmed by their presence.

Do they wear their clericals?

The seminarians are dressed clerically, but they wear a white lab coat which helps to blend them into the setting there. The patient looks at the seminarian but never notices the Roman collar. But then later on he realizes that "this is not one of the doctors; this is a clergyman." You know that sometimes when people are brought into a hospital emergency room and see a clergyman they immediately associate his presence with the danger of death. But here they had this fellow talking with them all along, easing their suffering and their anxieties, and explaining what is going on.

Do they talk to the patient about God?

In the emergency room they are not dealing with just Catholic persons, but with everybody who is brought in. Almost all the patients in this hospital are blacks, and many of them have close relations with Baptist and Methodist churches. So it is not too difficult or unusual in the emergency room to bring up the question of religion with the person and get them talking about God. So each one of the students, and also each one of the patients, has his own way of approaching religion. At first the students just follow along with me and watch what I do, but after a while they realize that they could just be themselves, as I was being myself, and utilize whatever opportunities arose for opening up the conversation. You might talk about everything under the sun before you get to talk about religion. It might take a couple of hours. They have the time because in the emergency room setting, people don't just move in and right out again. It's slow service in a public hospital like this.

There are other situations, of course, when the motion may be a little more rapid, particularly in the case of a severe trauma and the patient is unconscious. Here you don't have much time for the person who is in shock, had a bad accident, or was shot or stabbed, or has taken an overdose perhaps. But the majority of people in there are fairly alert and they can recognize by your presence that you are interested in them. You try to relieve some of their anxiety. Alleviating fear is one of the biggest things in the emergency room, because people don't know what is in store for them. Even at that point you can invite them to pray for God's blessings.

You say you are here primarily to minister to Catholic patients. How do you sort them out?

As patients come into the hospital I know that they are there within one hour of their admission. Once I find that a person is listed as a Catholic, I make out a census card on them. I feel that if you are going to help people you have to know them. That means that I've got to visit them and ask questions of them, not just walk in and wait for them to open up to me. They don't mind telling you. Everybody likes to talk about himself. The census card has a kind of spiritual history besides name, address, age, hospital room, day of admission, and date of previous admission. Beneath all that I have symbols to designate if they are married—validly or invalidly—if they're single, divorced, separated, been confirmed, and receive the sacraments with any degree of regularity.

We are here to help people spiritually, and I go right in

and get to the point and ask all those questions. A lot of the students find this difficult. They are young seminarians going to people much older than themselves, and they are often reluctant to ask questions of that kind. I insist on it—after all, the doctor has to know certain physical facts about patients—and I say, "You can't possibly do your spiritual job with somebody unless you know him. You don't have time to waste. If you decide to do it the next time, he may be discharged by then, or maybe dead."

You are the first one who has told me this. Don't you get resistance from the patients?

No, not with the patients, never. The reason is that Catholics feel that the priest has a right to know this information; and I don't think that black Catholics are any different on this than other Catholics. I realize that some of the experts in hospital pastoral care now insist that you mustn't ask the patients anything until they are ready to meet you on their level. My feeling is that that's a mistake. I don't want to criticize anybody, but to me that's a cop-out. At least, this is my own method that I developed in more than fifteen years' experience. By the end of the training year all of my students are firmly convinced that this is the way it ought to be done.

It's important to get people talking about themselves and their family. I ask them about their children, how many they have, and whether they are being raised in the Catholic religion. I ask them about going to Mass and receiving Communion. In this way you are opening up areas in their lives that are possible sources of anxiety for that person. When they're in the hospital they've got nothing but time on their hands. They're going to be thinking; they're going to be worried about the kids at home, and maybe about themselves because of what they haven't been doing. These are things you can talk with the patient about on subsequent visits. My first visit is usually very short and businesslike, and I get the questions out of the way that everybody hates to ask.

Do your trainees ever make these initial visits to patients?

As the only priest here, I have to take that responsibility. One of the big advantages for the students is that the vital information is now on the census cards, and I simply hand the seminarian my deck of cards for the ward he is working. By this time he has learned how to interpret the census card and has an idea at what point he can get into a conversation with the patient. Not only that, but he knows exactly which room and which patient to visit. You can't possibly remember everything about everybody. He can put all the census cards for an entire floor in his pocket and go from one room to the next.

After you get into the room how do you bring Christ to them?

I think as much as anything just by your presence. Yesterday I visited a sick lady I've known for a long time. When I walked in the room her face just brightened and she broke into tears; she was so pleased to see me. In fact, she remarked, "Your coming to see me is like the Lord coming in." Now that was simple because she is a believer and a friend. But then you have other people who aren't believers. We get quite a few Black Muslims into this hospital. I'd go into a room looking for a Catholic patient, but he has been moved to another room. Instead, in that bed was somebody else who turned out to be a Muslim. You could see he wanted nothing to do with me under these circumstances, and there was nothing I could do for him. Whenever I meet these Muslims I feel that it is a challenge not only to me, but to the Church. I make it a point to go back and see that person, just to say, "How are you doing today? Are you still having a lot of pain? I hope it'll soon be gone."

This has happened a number of times. I would just keep on going back, and before they are discharged from the hospital, we would be talking on friendly terms. In that way I think I was bringing Christ even to non-Christians. You show real concern about their bodily pain and suffering. I always remember Dorothy Day's remark, "We must minister to people's bodies in order to reach their souls." Sometimes I get into serious discussions with other patients who are non-Catholics. They would want to talk, or perhaps ask questions of a priest. Often you go in to see patients and you hardly have to say anything yourself. They do all the talking. In a sense they are preaching to themselves, talking about Jesus and about his role in their lives. That's usually a Baptist, because you know that this city hospital is about ninety-nine percent black, and you find a real depth of religion among them. Honestly, there are many times I go into a room to be of some help to somebody, and I come out feeling that I myself have been helped.

Tell me about the doctors you work with.

I live in the doctors' residence, have my meals with them in the same dining room, and we are just elbow to elbow all the time. They are all kinds: residents and interns and some of them professors. I know them all, and they know me. They send for me often, and they look for me to help them. They all know the students in the emergency room and appreciate their presence there. It doesn't matter if they are seminarians or sisters or deacons or the wives of deacons. They know what we are there for, and they feel that we are doing the job well.

Many of these physicians aren't Christians at all. We have Moslem doctors from the Middle East, and we have a lot of interns from India, Pakistan, Iraq, and Africa. They give us no trouble from the point of view of religion. I think the reason for their friendliness is that the interns mirror the attitudes of the residents. These foreigners have increased in numbers in recent years to get better medical training than they can get at home. Since I am already in close communication with the regulars on the medical staff, these interns fall right in line and imitate them. They haven't been any problem at all. I don't take any credit for this smooth relationship with the medical staff. After all, there was a Catholic chaplain in this hospital for over fifty years. So, all these men who preceded me helped to pave the way up to the present. I tell the

pastoral care students that if you show the least bit of interest
in what the doctor is doing he will do all he can to help you.

We have access to all the medical records and to the patients' charts. We are asked to read them in order to compre-
hend what is going on. In their lectures to the students the
doctors explain what happens in radiation therapy, or what
happens in the person having a heart attack. I am convinced
from experience—without being a medical doctor—that some
comprehension of the patients' medical problems puts us in
a better position to help them spiritually. So we are always
welcome to the physicians. The priest chaplain is always a
member of the so-called tumor board, reviewing cases of people who have cancer. In other words, the pastoral care people
are considered part of the team effort in treating the sick.

Let me tell you about the Jewish doctor who helped me
hear somebody's confession. He spoke Spanish and the patient spoke Spanish, but I didn't. The two of us were wheel-
ing the patient to the intensive care unit, and as we were
going down the corridor he began asking the patient the spiritual things I needed to know such as "When was the last
time you went to confession?" and he passed the word on to
me. He knew as much about it as any Catholic. He had gone
from kindergarten all the way through university in Catholic
schools. He knew all about the seal of confession and that the
patient could just say that he was sorry for all his serious sins.
At the end he told the patient I would give him absolution,
and he added, "Now don't forget to say the act of contrition."

What good things can you say about the nursing staff?

The first thing I say is that they are terribly overworked.
In a public hospital like this a nurse may have to take care of
fifteen or sixteen patients at once. That means to change
dressings, clean wounds, take blood pressure, check temperature, give blood transfusions, and, of course, give medication and consult with the doctors. Some of her patients
may be on mechanical ventilators and require closer attention. With experience they cope well with the multiple demands of patient care, but they dislike the paperwork,

keeping records and filling out forms, that the registered nurse now has to do.

We have more turnover than we should and a continuing shortage of nurses who, in my opinion, don't get adequate pay. But they are appreciative of us in pastoral care. I guess it's mainly because they see us frequently, but they see very few Protestant ministers here on a regular schedule of patient visitation. Whenever they have workshops for the nurses' in-service training they invite me to participate in it. In my earlier years here I would say that about thirty percent of the nurses, both black and white, were Catholic, but now they are almost all black; only a few are Catholic.

With a few exceptions, I judge them to be both fine nurses and devout Christians. Frequently I have come across nurses openly praying with their patients. I have the impression that nurses generally, at least those here in the hospital, are more religious, or spiritual, or pious, than most other people are. If the patients show any sign of a religious nature, such as praying out loud in their pain, the nurse responds to that. She would go along with that and perhaps help them to pray a bit more. I believe they bring Christ to the patient by their own goodness and compassion; it is their own way of witnessing to Christ. They might mention, for example, how much God means to them in their own life and work, and they want to bring God into the lives of the patients. Sometimes, even when they are with non-Christian patients, you discover nurses talking to them about God and getting the patient talking about his understanding of God. These are the things that I have witnessed myself.

What is your final word about your work?

There is no final word, except the need for many more pastoral care people in the hospital apostolate, especially in these big public hospitals. We ought to have more ministers representing the other denominations to care for all the non-Catholics. This is an extremely vital kind of work for a priest, and for me it's more satisfying than teaching and parish ministry. In the hospital setting you are doing what you are ordained to do. You're here to minister to people, to give them spiritual support, prayer and the sacraments. You help them move through their pain and suffering to get closer to God. This is just a wonderful experience.

Let me go back for a moment to my efficient system of census cards. By the time the patient is discharged from the hospital those cards contain a wealth of information. I never throw them away because many patients are repeaters. When they come back the second or third time I recognize them almost invariably and pick up again our relationship. If they continue to live in this city, they'll be back here at the end of their life and be received by a priest, either me or my successor, who knows them.

X

Nursing Is
More Than Techniques

Head nurse Elizabeth has long experience in an urban 370-bed Catholic
general hospital

What is your position at this hospital?

I am head nurse on a thirty-bed medical unit, which is
one of two wards on this floor. I have been here almost four-
teen years. Most of the patients on this unit are elderly, sixty
to eighty years old, a lot of terminally ill people with diag-
noses like cancer or people who have had massive strokes.
Generally the prognosis is extremely grave, even though they
are not all of them necessarily immediately terminal.

Did you get any training to meet the spiritual needs of patients?

Yes, that was pretty much part of our course content all
the way through in a very Catholic situation and atmosphere.
I got my nurse's training and a bachelor of science in nursing,
both under the auspices of a sisters' college that has since
gone out of existence. It was at the time of the Vatican Council
when all the rules were still in force. In the dormitories they
had us on our knees praying at eight o'clock every night in a
community fashion. We had a lot of church services, like

Mass every day and Benediction twice a week. It was a very Catholic environment, and maybe that's why it folded. I can't imagine college students and student nurses doing that now, but I understand that places like Oral Roberts and Bob Jones still do it.

Religious practices and the spiritual care of patients are to me part and parcel of the same, and they are all kind of intermingled in life. In almost any course we had as students we might end up discussing religion, or how the topic under discussion might affect morality, or be affected by it. It was a fine preparation for completeness, for the holistic under-standing of patient care that we hear so much about. All this helps us in dealing with the elderly and dying people up here. As far as taking care of dying patients that's something I myself and my staff deal with quite a bit here.

Does that cause you personal stress and strain?

Most of us get used to it and stay on the job. If you can't take it you move to some other kind of nursing. About a year ago my mother died very abruptly in a hospital near here. That was something I'd always dreaded because I had never lost anyone close to me. I spent a lot of time figuring out what my feelings were. My mother had kind of predicted that she would die when she did. She had a vision, or a dream—she was a very religious person, and I don't mean to make her sound like a weirdo—about a year and a half before she died. In her vision she said she was reading her own obituary in the newspaper on a certain date in October, and she actually died on October 1.

It's been my experience four or five times that when pa-tients tell me they're going to die, even though they don't look as though death is imminent, they usually die. The pa-tients who told me that, I didn't know well enough to get into any lengthy discussion with them about it, but they seemed very peaceful and accepting of the whole thing. They would tell me, "Today I'm going to die; I just know I am." So that when my mother told me that, I had the feeling it would hap-pen. It isn't that she wanted to die. She had a gastric ulcer, and the doctor kept putting off the care of it. She tried to prevent it happening, but she kind of knew it was going to happen. The professional part of myself said, "That's very likely to happen." But I didn't let her know that's where I was coming from. I went through real soul-searching for about a year and a half before she died. She did indeed die exactly as she had said, but she didn't will it. She was fifty-nine and didn't seem sick enough or old enough to die.

I tried to figure the whole thing out in my mind. I had to find out what my feelings were and work them out about death. It's one thing to take care of a patient who is dying; it's another thing to lose somebody who has been very close to you. You really have to figure this out for yourself—what dying is all about. I am basically a religious person but not the kind of person who goes to Mass every day. I go to Mass once a week on Sundays, but to me life should be kind of a continuous prayer, a continuous act of faith, and I regard it now as the natural course of events. God puts you on earth to do certain things; at least, he gives you the opportunity to do certain things. When that time has passed, then it's your turn to go for your day of reckoning. It's not a hostile thing. To me it's not like a challenge that you go before a hostile God.

Are you afraid of death?

I think I have the same amount of fear that anybody does about the unknown, not having been there myself. I was very afraid at the time when I was facing it in regard to my mother. But about a week before she died I had come to the point that whatever the Lord wanted I could accept it. I could resign myself to the whole thing, with one exception, that she ended up dying all by herself, all alone. I have feelings about what we do to patients in the hospital, bringing them out of their own home environment into an alien environment, stripping them of all their emotional supports—letting them face something like that, or the possibility that something like that might happen. We only let them have visitors by some arbitrary regulation about the hours for visits. The longer I experience this the more I favor home care and a hospice program.

With these older patients I see two kinds of dying: either the people who suddenly die in front of me and we try to revive them, or people who are dying gradually and are really not aware of the fact that they are dying. I have watched people go the whole gamut, from the "There's nothing wrong with me. Just a little anemia, or something." When they are told that they have a terrible diagnosis they continue to deny it for a while, and they get very hostile and angry. Sometimes this goes on for months without drifting into all the five stages that Kübler-Ross talked about.

Do you see spirituality as a way of relieving pain and anxiety?

I think it's very important to a lot of our patients. We have five or six older sister visitors assigned here from the Daughters of Charity. Some repeater patients come back every six months, or every year, and the first thing they want to know is who is assigned to their floor. They all have religious medals on, even if they are not Catholics. They dearly look forward to these sisters coming to visit. They don't just talk about the weather or bits of gossip. They do end up talking seriously about religion. Most of our patients are black people and they are overtly very religious. On Sundays there's a lot of chanting and a lot of people come from their churches and hold services in the room. Practically all day long it is a parade of people in their white dresses, deacons and deaconesses. There are about ninety percent black patients here.

These are semi-private rooms, and there are usually three or four people from the patient's church. Often the other patient in the room may not be alert enough, in which case there is no problem, or the other patient may go out and sit in the solarium. I don't remember that I ever really had a problem with this, and I feel it's good for the patients. Usually people are very accepting of other people's religious needs, especially in an environment like this.

Are the sister visitors retired nurses?

Some of them may have been nurses, but I don't believe that has any bearing on what they do. They get little computer sheets every morning. They have assigned units they go to, and they know who is on the list for their unit. They'll go around and visit these patients, but they also visit patients who have been transferred off their unit to another unit. They bring little things to the patients. They come up with Mother Seton scapulars, and medals and holy pictures. They are very willing to talk religion to anybody, no matter what their faith. They sort of play it by ear depending on where the patient is coming from. They come and ask us about certain patients and how bad off they are. We can't give them detailed information, but they get kind of a working knowledge of what the case is.

There is one sister who is called an ombudsman, a younger lady who tries to allay people's initial fears in this very emotional setting. She's out there in the visitors' lounge with the relatives and then back in with the patient, and then back out again to follow them around. There are a couple of them also who are younger. If we have an arrest in the middle of the night—I don't know where they are then—but they appear out of the woodwork. They are willing to do anything that is needed, and they make it a point also to spend a lot of time with the relatives of patients.

I'm not sure what kind of training these sisters have, but they have monthly meetings with the chaplain's department. We have two priests here who are around the clock and who live here at the hospital. The nurses cooperate with them, and they cooperate with the sister visitors. As far as I can see this arrangement takes good care of the religious and spiritual needs of patients.

Do the nurses feel they are helping to meet spiritual needs?

The definition of nursing is not limited only to their technical skills. Nursing is an art of getting to communicate with the patient and getting to know where he's really coming from. To be a really good nurse you have to be able to get them to talk to you, and to verbalize everything that's bothering them. You may not be religious yourself, but you're able to appreciate their kind of religion and get them the help that they need. But there's a fine line: you can't wind up getting involved. You can't go too far and get too close to them because then you are not always very therapeutic. You can wind up trying maybe to meet some of your own needs.

I have several nurses, for example, who are drop-away Catholics. I have some who are younger and unsure of themselves and are trying to work out their own religious convictions. I have people who have not worked out all their feelings about death and dying and suffering. They are very concerned about this and they get very close to their patients, but they have to be able to continue functioning; they can't let themselves just fall apart. I don't want them to be just technically oriented, but I don't want them coming here to take care of patients just to meet their own needs.

Nurses are here primarily for the patient. Not that there can't be some reciprocal aspects of it, but they have to realize that their primary focus is for the patient. Sometimes you have to pull away a little bit in order to be able to keep going. This summer I had a very heavy group of patients, for about three months, who were dying. Two or three of them were very alert and knew that they were dying, and were very religious. They belonged to all kinds of religious groups, who came in from the outside to visit them. Toward the end of the summer, shortly before they died, they really got to some of my people because they had absorbed all this suffering for so long.

I'm proud of my people here because they were able to take it and carry on. Sometimes I think we die a little bit when the patient dies. If you're taking care of sixteen patients, and they're all suffering and dying, it has an effect on you. One of my nurses literally cried her way through about a month of this. She said, "I walk out of here when I go home, and I see that they each need eighty things times sixteen persons, not just from a physical point of view, but to help them handle all their problems." Trying to handle that situation every day, she just got to the point emotionally where she said, "I'm just not able to do it all. I just can't absorb all of this." What happened is that it would come out in the form of tears.

Are doctors ever affected this way?

The doctors are the greatest ones for running away from anything like that. A lot of times I'll ask them for something I think the patient needs and they'll say to me, "Hasn't he died yet?" And they'll joke about somebody who is really suffering. I think it's their way of handling their own feelings. They feel that they can't do anything to end the misery any earlier, and they are kind of stuck. We have to realize that the oncologists here deal with dying patients on a routine basis, and they're often frustrated that there is no cure.

I have reminded several of them that they come in here to see the patient and they stay at most five minutes. I've said to them, "And then you leave while the nurse is in there for an eight-hour shift every day." In some respects, my people become defenders and champions of the patients, and they'll ask for stronger drugs than the doctor wants to prescribe. There are a couple of patients the doctors would classify as comatose, which is supposed to mean that they don't hurt so much. But I ask for the right to give them really strong narcotics, and the doctors are reluctant. We are the ones who have to watch the patients who can't talk, whom nobody visits, and who scream with pain. I don't mean that the physicians are hard-hearted individuals, but they have this thing about addiction even when they have patients who will never get better.

We've been talking only of the dying. Tell me about patients who get well and go home.

We spend a lot of time doing discharge planning, which is the formal way we have to make contact with the family of the patient. Right from the beginning, when a patient comes in we have to sit down and talk with the families to let them know what's going on. This is now being required in the

Lincoln Christian College

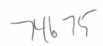

nursing profession, and we have to do it in order to maintain our JCAH accreditation, that's with the Joint Commission for Accreditation of Hospitals. It's one of the groups who gives us our license.

The discharge planning is really an attempt to assure that the patient will have care after leaving the hospital. So, we have to assess the patients, where they're coming from in all respects, and what the family situation is. You start from there trying to meet their needs, both in the hospital and after they leave here, no matter whether they are going to a nursing home or back with their own family. With the federal cutbacks there's a significant lack of money for follow-up care of the elderly—I think probably more so here than in other places because we have a lot of poor people in the inner city. We invite the families of patients to come in and help with patient care just so they know what to do and will feel comfortable when they get the patient home. So, we get to know some of these families very well because we have a lot of patients who come back. I had one patient that I've taken care of forty-five times, and, of course, she finally died.

When you have patients who are repeaters, the family comes out frequently and verbalizes a lot about the patient. It depends on who they are and how close you get to them whether they end up talking about religion. It's really the nurse who spends more time with them than the sister visitors or the chaplains, and most of my people would pick up on that. People are living older and older, and they're going home with multiple diseases, things that you have to care for in the home. The family members have to work out their feelings, for instance, when they look at a colostomy for the first time, or something like that. We have to teach the family members how to take care of the patient who goes home from here. Professional after-care in the home by nurses and social workers is much too expensive for most of our patients.

What are your concluding comments to wrap up this conversation?

You've been pushing me to be specific about the spiritual and religious approach to the sick, and I have to admit that it is difficult and it's intangible. It's a very hard thing, you know, to describe. It's a very taxing situation for the nurses when you are trying to relate to somebody so totally, to meet whatever their needs are. Sometimes we have to become the reason why the patient wants to go on living, at least for a period of time. Then we try to bring them back into the real world. We are different things to different people, and it depends too on the individual capabilities of the nurse, because nursing is much more than technical knowledge and behavior.

My people here are professionally and technically well trained nurses, but some of them are pretty fuzzy about religion themselves. Some of them who are Catholics will laugh about going to church. They seem to be in a kind of religious quandary themselves; maybe they are sincerely trying to work things out for themselves. It seems to be the mood of the day to laugh about religion because God and religion are not uppermost on their minds. But they do respond to people's religious needs. You just can't separate it; you have to treat everything.

What it comes down to in practice is that you can't draw the fine line between the spiritual and the physical. On the other hand you are only fifty percent of a nurse if you concentrate only on the physical and technical tasks, because in many cases the other fifty percent means everything. You can do all the technical and physical things, and it doesn't amount to a row of pins if you are not really giving them the emotional and spiritual support. The religious support has to be what the patient needs, not what the nurse needs.

XI

Everyone Knows
the Lord's Prayer

Father James is a Jesuit priest, diocesan coordinator of health affairs in a
rural area of the country

*How does one become a coordinator of health affairs in a Catholic
diocese?*

In my own case this title was conferred upon me by the
bishop to perform tasks above and beyond my regular job as
head chaplain at a 300-bed non-sectarian, non-profit hospital.
Maybe I got the appointment on the basis of seniority. I've
been at it consecutively longer than any other priest in the
diocese; for eight years I was with the Veterans' Administration hospital, and for the last eight years at my current assignment. I got certified back in 1970 under a kind of
grandfather clause, on the basis of age and experience as a
Jesuit priest, when the Veterans' Administration hospital
sent me off for a two-week program that they called a "Chaplains' School." In formal and official terms I was certified by
the National Association of Catholic Chaplains.

What do you do as coordinator?

It is an interesting fact that we have only two Catholic
general hospitals in the diocese, both of them operated by re-

ligious orders of sisters and well-staffed with good pastoral care departments. So I meet with them only as a consultant from time to time when they have something to discuss. My main task at the present time is to get chaplains into the eighteen other hospitals in this diocese. The bishop is concerned that Catholic patients are in these non-Catholic hospitals without adequate pastoral care coverage. We have succeeded in establishing a pastoral care department in six of the hospitals, but the others now still make arrangements with the priests in the neighboring parishes to visit the sick. This is true also of the Protestants who have to depend on the personal schedule their minister can set with the hospital administrators. My ultimate aim is to have certified and trained chaplains, both Catholic and Protestant, in every one of them.

Most of these hospitals are non-profit as well as non-sectarian, with the exception of two that are proprietary. My repeated argument with them is that "you can't be a first-class hospital if you don't provide pastoral care for the patients." No administrator I have met with so far denies this statement, but they want the churches to provide the clergyman and pay his expenses. I argue that the hospital should think highly enough of the welfare of their sick patients that they pay the salary for a permanent chaplaincy. We are making some slow progress in that direction, but meanwhile I prod the local ministers and priests to take some responsibility for the hospitalized members of their congregations. I urge them also to get their lay people involved in this ministry.

Have you had any success with the laity?

One of the best organizations in the county is an interdenominational group called Church Women United, with branches in most of the localities. I got to their leaders and helped them establish the United Volunteers. We now have them pretty well organized in every locality where there is a hospital, and they are also utilized in the hospitals that have pastoral care departments. You could almost say that they are the heart of the ministry to the sick, not only because they personally visit the patients but also because they pave the way, or open the pathway, for the clergy.

Let me tell you how this works at my hospital. The women of Volunteers United work out a schedule so that one or more are assigned daily to visit the thirty or so new arrivals we get every day. At the front desk they pick up the new cards. Catholics take the Catholics; the Protestant women take all the rest. At our hospital there are sixty volunteers who rotate on a weekly basis; they are blacks as well as whites, and in our case we also have a half dozen retired laymen who do the visiting. They are most faithful. Since we began this program of visiting there has not been even one day without the lay people visiting the patients.

Without these volunteers we simply could not do an adequate job of hospital chaplaincy; with them, nobody gets neglected. They make the initial visit to the patient and are always mindful that this is a church ministry. They give us a reflection of the type of person we are going to visit, if indeed they think we should visit them. For example, we have enough extraordinary eucharistic ministers, both male and female, who can bring Communion to them. Some patients aren't satisfied with that and they want to see their priest or their minister. We get hints from the lay visitors about the attitude of the patient, for instance, if they seem to be turned off by the church or by the clergy. For example, we get a signal when the patients say, "I don't want to go to the sacraments," and the visitor puts a code mark on the card.

Are you saying that you are selective in the patients the chaplain visits?

Well, some people have priority. For instance, the clergyman sees every person who is going to have surgery; and the nurses and doctors know this priority and always cooperate with us. Or if the person has had a serious accident, as soon as he's brought to the emergency room we get a call. We also single out elderly people and give them special attention. We have to do some screening because there are too many patients for the number of clergy we have. The turnover is about ten percent every day, and we just couldn't reach them all.

It may seem a calculated way of doing hospital ministry, and I admit the ideal situation would be one in which ministers make a leisurely call on their sick parishioners and have no concern about the amount of time each visit takes. The fact is that we are forced to set up priorities based on the degree of spiritual needs we perceive. You don't hesitate about patients who are old or in danger of death from illness or accident. That's where the chaplain goes first. Then the next level of priority is for those who are more in spiritual danger than in physical danger. Often when we say that a patient "needs a chaplain" we are talking about somebody who is at odds with God, who needs to "get back" to the sacraments or to the kind of spiritual peace the minister of religion can bring.

You can call this selectivity if you want to, but it is the most reasonable and efficient system we have been able to devise. And in a sense it really functions to cover everybody because the lay volunteers make that universal initial contact with every patient. Of course we slip up sometimes, and on occasions the volunteer may not be as alert as she should be, but we have here one aspect of the lay apostolate. The lay church members are making a genuine contribution to the work of the Lord; they are directly helping the clergy in restoring or strengthening human relationships with the Creator.

You said some patients don't want to see the chaplain.

These also come in several varieties. Oddly enough, some people are hesitant about seeing the chaplain because they don't want their own parish priest or pastor to visit them. We don't ask them why, because that's their business. The lay visitor may pick up another kind of message which suggests that "I can't go to the sacraments because I was married by the judge." We instruct the volunteers not to probe into the attitudes and problems of the patient, but we do get from them some notions about the receptivity of the patient to the visit of the chaplain, especially if one case seems more urgent than others. Volunteers need experience; so do the chaplains.

There is only one time that I can think of that I was turned away from a patient who did not want me to pray for him in his room. I tried to kid him along but he wouldn't budge, and I said, "I wouldn't go against your wishes, sir, but when I go outside this room I'm going to say a little prayer for you, and you won't be able to stop me." He smiled and said, "No, I can't " I waited a couple of days and then came back to see how he was feeling. Then on the third visit he began to thaw out and talk more, and we had some good conversations. Before he was discharged from the hospital he had worked out a nice relationship with God.

I don't think I have ever found a person who was really turned off from God. This is where, I think, patients in the hospital want somebody to help them renew their relationship with God. Very few people are completely out of touch with reality, and one of the realities of life is the mystery of God's presence everywhere. So they want to get in contact with that. It often happens that it is not through your own religion. If I go into a ward and I bless the Catholic party, some patient in another bed who is not a Catholic will say, "Father, would you give me a blessing too?"

In one instance I was anointing a man in the Veterans' Administration hospital, and when I finished I said, "Now, let's say the Lord's Prayer." Well, there were three other buddies, or veterans, in that ward, and before I got halfway through the Lord's Prayer every man had joined in and was praying with the sick man, with the man who was dying. It was really a revelation to me how everybody joined in with the man who needed prayer. They were of different church denominations. From then on, the Lord's Prayer meant a whole lot more to me than it had ever before because I saw it as a kind of universal and ecumenical prayer.

Do the priests deal with non-Catholic patients?

Well, the needs of the sick persons have to be balanced against the importance of good ecumenical relations across denominational lines. There are still some rural fundamentalist preachers around here who are antagonistic to other clergy, especially Catholic priests. But things are changing; even the Baptists get along with us pretty well. To answer your question: yes, sometimes we visit with a very sick person if his or her minister is not available. We had one case where a rabbi had a heart attack and was dying, but they couldn't locate his back-up rabbi. The charge nurse called and said, "I think you should talk with this man; he's dying." She seemed to think the nearest thing to a rabbi is a Catholic priest.

You know, the first thing this Jewish clergyman asked me was, "Father, what's going to happen to me after I die? Will I die like an animal that just disappears?" I said, "No, when you die God is going to reward all of your good actions; and if you have done anything that offended God and are sorry for it now, he is going to forgive you because he loves you." His face brightened up, and we talked a little more because he was so weak, but we said some universal prayers like, "Almighty God, help me in my hour of need." The thought of the loving and forgiving Father in heaven seemed to console him. Here I was the Catholic priest and he was the Jewish rabbi, and that conversation was good for me too. I have never forgotten that question: "What's going to happen to me when I die?"

Over the years I've ministered to Muslims, to Buddhists and to Hindus, and all of them have a strong belief in the Supreme Being. They may not call him God the same as we do in the western world. They might call him Allah or by some other title, but they all believe in some kind of Supreme Being and they want to be in contact with the Supreme Being. That's a universal fact that I have experienced among the sick and dying. The only time you might find people who didn't want to be in contact with the Creator is if they are out of contact with reality. If they're rational and know what they are doing, I don't find any atheists among them. They have some kind of belief in a future life, but they don't know exactly what it's going to be. But then we don't know that ourselves.

How do you deal with Catholics who stopped going to church?

It's a funny thing about these people who usually are quite friendly with the priest chaplain—as long as you're not from their parish. That seems to be true of Protestants too. Most often—and I found this from experience—they have had a run-in with some clergyman. I even ask them if they've had a problem with their priest, and I'll say, "Well, I'm here to apologize for that; and you know that even we priests can make a mistake sometimes. When you say the Lord's Prayer you have to forgive your enemies, and when you say that part of the prayer 'Forgive us our trespasses' I think you ought to forgive that priest, and don't hold it against God because a human priest has made a human mistake." That works almost all the time.

There are other reasons why they don't want to talk to the chaplain. A lot of them say, "I don't go to church because I don't want to be a hypocrite." When they say that I usually give them the off-the-cuff definition of a hypocrite. I tell them it means that you don't live up to your highest beliefs. I'll put out my hand and say, "Shake, because here's another hypocrite too; I don't always live up to my highest ideals." By that time I see them smiling, and before we get through our conversation they have usually broken down the barriers. Another time a man didn't want to be reunited with God because he said he had broken every commandment in the book. I said, "Well, you must be worse than the good thief on the cross." He said, "No, Father, I'm not worse than the good thief." I said, "You know, the Lord forgave the good thief, and if you're not worse than he is, you can be sure that the Lord is ready to forgive you. He loves you just as he loved the thief on the cross."

Do you have good relations with the medical staff?

Before I came to City General there was no regular full-time pastoral care department, and the doctors didn't have daily contact with the same experienced chaplains. I'm not sure what that means except that both the clergy and the doctors were dealing with each other as strangers, and they were strangers. When I first came here I didn't have too good a relationship with the physicians because only a few of them were closely known to the Jesuits and myself. Even though about sixty percent of them are Catholics they kind of stayed in the wings as though the priest might pronounce some new doctrine that would interfere with their medicine.

What happens then is that your relationship with the medical staff grows with the length of time you are working in the hospital, just as happens with any other team of which you are a member. After a while we develop a personal friendship so that they invite me out to their homes for dinner. I am now a member of the medical ethics commission at the hospital, and I regularly give the invocation for their meetings and conferences. On one occasion, after I gave the invocation at a doctors' banquet, I took my place at the table next to a doctor friend who is not a Catholic. He said, "You know, Father, you praised the doctors very highly in your invocation. We're really not all that good." And then I said, "Well, doctor, maybe that's something for you all to shoot at."

Do they consult you on ethical questions?

Yes, but I think more often they know what they are going to do, and they know it's ethical, but they seem to want moral support. For example, we had a baby patient, born prematurely, that I had to baptize right away. Only the nurse and the doctor were there with me, and he said, "Father, this baby has multiple deformities, and I'm at a loss what next step I should take. I could let nature take its course—feed the baby, take care of it, keep it comfortable until it dies." Then we had a little conference when I asked him what the alternative would be, what were the causes of the deformities, and what were the chances for correcting them successfully. He said there would have to be a series of surgical operations, because there were probably as many internal malformations as external: "By the time I get through cutting the baby it would most likely be worse off than before I started." This was a professional medical opinion, and we both formed the professional ethical opinion that it would be right, as we said, "to let nature take its course."

In another case the ethical question was discussed with the patient himself who was in deep depression. He had been on the dialysis machine for four years and there was no hope for improvement. In fact, he was getting worse and weighed less than a hundred pounds. The only way he continued to live was on this artificial machine because he had no kidneys. He was ready to give up, but someone had told him he would be committing suicide if he stopped the dialysis treatment. The nurse called me to see him, and when I did I met his brother who talked more than he did. Then we had a conference with his mother and his son, together with his doctor; so we all came to the same conclusion, agreeing with the patient that he did not have to continue the process. He seemed much less depressed when I told him that God was calling him home, and he died in peace.

Do you deal with the relatives of patients?

There again the nurses are the ones who see the family just as they are with the patient more than anybody else, but even before the nurse, we will get to deal with the relatives when there has been a serious accident and the patient comes out of the emergency room. A non-Catholic nurse told me that a few words from a clergyman calms down a frantic relative better than any sedative or any hypo. She said, "We've seen cases here where we were trying to calm down relatives after an accident and couldn't do anything with them, but as soon as they saw the priest come and start to pray, everything simmered down and they became quiet."

This is where you experience people getting plugged into reality with relationship to the Creator. That's the main thing with the whole spiritual ministry to the sick and suffering, being plugged in with the Creator. Another case I had in the emergency room—a lady's husband was in a serious accident, and the doctor told her he could not save him. She was crying, "Why does God do this to me?" We said the Lord's

Prayer together, and she simmered down for a while, but then she started up again. We said another prayer, but she kept repeating, "Why does God do this to me?" Finally, I couldn't think of anything else, so I said, "You know, my dear, there was another woman whose close relative was dying on a cross, and she didn't ask God that question, 'Why are you doing this to me?' " That was like an inspiration because she did calm down.

I should have asked you this in the beginning: Why did you go into this kind of ministry in the first place?

I wish I could say that it was my tremendous compassion for sick and suffering humanity that brought me to this work, but that came afterward with more and more experience. I have to say that it was a less emotional attraction to the work. I was convinced that medicine was becoming so technical and mechanistic that it had no place for God, or God was being shoved to the side. I think that's the main reason I'm still so interested, and every opportunity I get I want to say that we've got to bring God back to the field of medicine, to the hospitals, to the emergency room and the operating room, to intensive care and nursing. It is still my rational conviction that we ought to get God into the schools of medicine as well as into the hospital systems.

XII

Pastoral Ministry Is Everybody's Job

Sister Teresa is director of pastoral
ministry in an 800-bed urban Catholic
medical center

Do you see pastoral ministry as a specific religious calling?

It seems to have become specialized in the recent past,
but I think pastoral ministry is exactly what our sisters were
already doing when they opened this hospital over a century
ago. Nowadays we need an organized department of pastoral
ministry, because our large hospital staff is not able to do the
mission in this Catholic institution as it was originally envi-
sioned. When we were first established we recognized Jesus
Christ in every patient for whom we cared. That call and that
ministry has not changed; it is the same today as it was then.
If everyone on the hospital staff recognized the human dignity of all patients and treated them with Christ-like compassion we would have no need for a department of pastoral
ministry. We would have worked ourselves out of a job.

We say that the whole hospital—everybody who works
here in any capacity at all—is geared to the care and cure of
the suffering patients. It's a kind of ideal that may never become a reality. We've got too many people doing too many
different things, but I guess you can't run a hospital any other

way. In a sense, you have two kinds of people employed here: those who have direct contact with the patients and those who hardly ever see a patient. The ones who don't see the patients are in administrative positions, making decisions or doing office work, and also in the lower levels, custodians and housekeepers and cooks and laundry workers. These are the people—at the top and at the bottom of the system—that we have to energize and spiritualize, and convince them that they too are part of our mission. They share in the vocation of bringing Jesus to the sick and suffering.

One way of reaching all these employees is through the human dignity seminar conducted for a full day, from eight in the morning till four in the afternoon, every other week. We call this the mission ministry, the educational task of one of the sisters in the pastoral care department. As we look at it, the total mission of the hospital requires the communication of our philosophy of human dignity, and of the values underlying the commitment that the sisters had from the beginning in establishing this hospital. Our ministry concretizes this mission in our one-on-one experience of bringing people into the awareness of the presence of God in both the patients and in all who serve to help them get well.

Have you been able to organize the pastoral care department so that it reaches out to all parts of the hospital?

I learned the hard way with eight years' experience as the administrator of one of our smaller hospitals. I started off as a registered nurse with a bachelor's degree, and then became a clinical specialist in psychiatric nursing. I got a two-year leave of absence to do the ACPE program at a Baptist hospital in New England, but I realized that the four units of training were very psychologically oriented. Most of what I learned there I had already done for my master's program in psychiatric training. So I spent the second year of my leave studying theology with the Oblate Fathers. Let me emphasize that this hospital is run by the sisters, not by the medical staff. We get excellent cooperation from the doctors and other health care professionals, but everyone here has some sense of our Christian philosophy and mission.

My idea of pastoral ministry is that we minister to every person who is involved in our institution. This means not just the patient and the patient's family, but also the nurses and doctors, and all employees in all departments of the hospital. In some instances we pay more attention to staff than to patients. For example, the staff caring for the leukemia children tend to have tremendous frustrations, and the pastoral person spends a lot of time dealing with them individually, and also with the parents of the children. Another crucial area where we pay more attention to staff and employees than to patients is in our cooperation with the personnel department. Most of their work is routine, but we are called upon sometimes to handle disputes or to deal with an employee who is in some kind of trouble.

We like to think that we are at the service of an informal Christian congregation or community. Pastoral ministry reaches into all areas of the medical center, and each member of the pastoral care team acts as the "pastor" of a designated "parish." This means that the assigned areas of ministry are not limited only to the sick rooms of the patients but also to the laboratories and pharmacy, medical records, business office, dietary, laundry, housekeeping. The people in all these areas are entitled to the services of a hospital chaplain.

In a sense, they constitute territorial parishes, but I'd rather call them "personal" parishes because each of the eight chaplains on the team is responsible for a specific group of people. Besides myself, we have three full-time priest chaplains who are trained in clinical pastoral education, and four sisters who are full-time pastoral associates (we are not allowed to call them chaplains). They are also products of clinical pastoral education and are certified according to the criteria of the USCC. Of course, the department has a secretary and a sacristan. We also have five students in training under my supervision: one lay woman, two religious sisters and two religious brothers.

How big are the pastoral parishes?

If we average out the number of patients we would have one pastor to about eighty parishioners, because our census is down now to about seven hundred patients. But the ratio is very uneven. In the high turnover areas of surgery and intensive care and oncology and renal dialysis the pastoral staff-patient ratio might be one to about fifty patients. At the same time the pastoral person is dealing with doctors and nurses, social workers and dieticians, and everybody who is attending to those patients.

We have gradually worked out the assignments according to the variety of gifts and preferences of the pastoral ministers. One staff member who had previously been a teacher says, "I would not like to work entirely with children," while another prefers to be with the sick youngsters. Some areas of the hospital are more stressful than others and some staff members adapt more easily than others to stress. So we talk not only about the type of patients they like to work with but we also have to think of the non-patient areas. For instance, in the housekeeping department we have to have a pastoral person who is fluent in Spanish. Some of these workers can't read or write, and many of them speak and understand only Spanish.

It's part of our job also to relate to the patient's family and relatives, and in many instances that requires at least a conversational knowledge of Spanish. Almost seventy percent of the patients are of Mexican background. That's not to say that they don't know any English at all. We are fortunate that many of the nurses and other health-care personnel get along pretty well in Spanish. The same is true of the lay people who volunteer as special ministers of the Eucharist. We arrange a schedule that guarantees the services of three eucharistic ministers every day. One religious sister comes in from a neighboring parish six days a week. We have a husband-wife team that comes in on weekends. Others come twice a week. These people are here strictly for the distribution of Holy Communion and are not typical lay visitors.

Don't get me wrong about lay visitors. What I am looking

for now are several lay volunteers who have been trained as evangelizers. Our diocese has just begun a training program for lay people who can do the old-style kind of catechizing. The Baptists and Fundamentalists call it "witnessing" which is really the teaching of Christian doctrine. The majority of our patients say they are Catholics, but many of them don't really understand their relationship to their Creator. In our form of Hispanic culture here we recognize a basic need for evangelization. This is not a matter of proselytizing, or converting non-Catholics to the Church. It is a matter of helping Catholics to understand something about God and about God's love for them. Even in our well-organized pastoral team we don't have the time to supply this need, but we think that we can get some lay people involved to do it.

If everybody should be involved in pastoral ministry, do you really get the doctors interested in what you are doing?

Not all of them, and we are not completely successful, but I think we continue to make more impact all the time. Interestingly enough in this area—and I don't want to be a female chauvinist—I believe that the women physicians have a greater awareness than the males in the value of spirituality. As a matter of fact, just recently and on three occasions I had women physicians ask for prayer for patients. One of them had a child patient who was dying of cancer, and there was nothing else she could do. She wasn't a Catholic and wasn't sure what to ask for, but she wanted to know if we could have an "abbreviated Mass" in the child's room as he was dying. The Mass was a wonderful experience, and the boy received his First Communion. The physician was there with the family and the nurses.

Certainly the Catholic doctors—or most of them—know what we are trying to do in our spiritual ministry. Some of the non-Catholic doctors are at first a little puzzled by our approach, but they gradually take notice and develop respect. For example, there is always a pastoral care person present at the patient-care team conferences. It is understood that our pastoral "specialty" must be represented. In fact, we are the ones who push the practice of a weekly patient conference. In each unit the key people—doctors, nurses, social workers, physical therapists—must sit down with us once a week and discuss all the patients in the unit. This is real and immediate communication for the welfare of the patient. The physicians are becoming more and more interested in that procedure.

Another thing we have is an occasional team conference about the needs of some individual patient. The group is called together by anyone who has a question about the care of a patient in any area of the hospital. Is there something more, or different, we can be doing for the patient? Any one of us may request a patient-care conference to find an answer to such a question. Just two weeks ago we had a little boy of six who had been run over by a truck and was paralyzed from the neck down. The doctor called me about having a team conference to see what to do about this child. He couldn't breathe on his own; he had to have a machine. I had to be out of town and couldn't be there for the meeting. They were all there, including the parents, for the discussion of what the doctor feels, what the social worker feels, what the pastoral person feels, might be best for this patient. With the family input they had to make their decision, and you can imagine the tremendous struggle this was for everybody trying to reach an agreement in that room.

I haven't always seen mutual respect between the medical staff and the pastoral care team. You seem to have a good relationship here.

That's true, and part of the explanation goes back to the consistent policies the sisters have maintained over the years. For a long time it has been well known in the local medical profession that not every doctor can obtain affiliation with this medical center, nor does every doctor want to live up to our rules and expectations. Of course, every hospital medical staff has its own criteria for professional conduct, but the doctors here recognize something more than that. Our reputation rests not only on high moral and ethical principles but also on what you call mutual respect—I call it the spirit of love in a Christian community.

At the present time there is also a personal aspect about this relationship. In some hospitals I think the pastoral care people are a bit timid in relating to physicians, even when the doctors try not to be intimidating. I have the advantage of eight years' experience as a hospital administrator, and I have no hesitancy in dealing with the medical staff. More than that, I remind them that I am their pastor and they are members of my parish. They know that I too have had adequate professional training not only in clinical pastoral care but also in clinical psychiatric nursing.

This relationship seems to be working. They insisted that I represent them on the medicine and religion committee of the county medical society. That is where I learned to appreciate the excellence of our own situation. Some of the ministers from other hospitals have an antagonistic attitude toward physicians and vice versa. The doctors and the ministers hardly talk to each other, or if they do they seem to feel threatened by each other. I have the feeling that they don't understand the similarities of healing between religion and medicine, and they are frustrated in not being able to coordinate their roles. The committee on the county medical society was discouraged that they couldn't make any progress in the discussion, and some of them asked, "How do you do it at the medical center?" I get the feeling that they are sometimes envious of the smooth cooperation we enjoy among ourselves.

We haven't said much about nurses. Are they participating in your pastoral mission?

Most of them desire to, but they are now so highly technologically involved in patient care that it's difficult for them. As I become more and more knowledgeable in the pastoral ministry I come to see the tremendous resemblance between what I'm doing now as a pastoral person and what I did more than twenty years ago as an old-time sister supervisor of nurses on a ward. The nurses I worked with were mostly diploma nurses and technically very competent. As a religious sister I had more education, and I saw myself as a resource person technologically in nursing, but the majority of my time was spent in visiting the patients and in talking with the doctors and nurses about the patients.

My first assignment back then was in the intensive care unit, when they were starting to do tracheotomies and using machines for artificial respiration. I remember talking to families about having the patient taken off the machine, and that it would be okay for them to tell that to the doctor. Later on, the families would come back and thank me because their loved one had gone beyond the recognition of dignity. So I did that, and if a patient was dying in the middle of the night I would be called up to be with the children or with the spouse of the dying person. In other words, I was already doing pastoral care as a sister nurse, but we didn't call it that in those days when we thought that pastoral care meant only chaplains and sacraments. This is what inspires me to say that everybody working in the hospital should demonstrate the same kind of total care and concern that the sisters originally had in founding this hospital.

In this sense the concept of pastoral care is not new, but today there is more depth in that we do have special training, and we have to take more responsibility, and are more involved in decision-making. One of the big differences is that we did not have all those machines that extend the dying process. They are called life-sustaining machines, and the fact is that people would die sooner if they didn't have the machines on them. What this does really is to provide an extended grieving time for the family. When the family learns that there is no hope for the patient, they begin to grieve intensely and even begin to make plans for the funeral. But the longer the patient is on a machine, the longer that grief and anticipation lasts. I don't think any family should be subjected to that additional suffering.

Well, what are you doing about that here?

I have started on a study of our actual program of cardiopulmonary resuscitation. We have been doing about twenty to twenty-five CPR's a month, and the whole question is why we continue to have so many of them. The majority of these people die within forty-eight hours anyway. We have a long-standing committee on medicine and religion in our hospital medical staff. We have been wrestling with the technical procedures rather than with the moral question of using extraordinary means to keep a patient breathing. Of course, the doctors are sensitive to their obligations and they hate to see their patients die, but I think there's another factor at work here. My experience is that since the technology is available, the doctors simply say, "Let's use the technology." And they always want to give the patient "one last chance."

Now we are beginning to think more about the unnecessary pain we inflict on members of the family by adding to their grief. When the condition of the patient is irreversible, everyone knows that death is imminent, but the two parties who have to make the decision are the patient's physician and close relatives. People don't always think clearly in such situations. We had a man here on the machines for several days but his family was too excitable to reach a decision. For some reason they went to the judge here in town to get a court order to remove the machine. The judge called our executive director and asked him, "What's going on?" He said, "I figure you have some way of handling this." Of course, we immediately brought the doctor and the family together, and the patient was taken off the machine. Our medical center has the reputation for always doing the proper and ethical thing.

Our special committee on medicine and religion has decided that when patients are admitted to the hospital they should be told about the process of cardiopulmonary resuscitation and should be asked: "Do you want machines if your heart stops?" This takes the place of the so-called "living will." Many of the patients, especially the elderly, may say, "Oh no, I'm ready to go; I don't want the machines." Then we talk to the family and ask them to let the doctor know their decision because the doctor has to put it on the chart. In a sense, this puts the ultimate decision back on the physician, and some physicians are reluctant to take it. But I think the doctors are coming around to the realization that we don't have to call for the resuscitation of everybody who is dying.

You seem to be dealing with medical ethics as much as with spiritual ministry. Is that true?

The traditional problems of medical ethics have been clarified and settled by the traditional principles of respect for the value of human life. For example, everyone here knows that sterilization and abortion are moral evils. The ethical obligation of all hospital personnel is to care for people who are sick and suffering, with the intention of restoring them as fully as possible to good health. That sounds like the textbook and does not touch the many specific ethical questions the physician has to answer: whether to perform a surgical operation, what type of medication to prescribe, and the most common contemporary problem of machines that we have already discussed.

In some sense, I think all of these ethical decisions have a spiritual dimension because we acknowledge that everything we do is done in the service of the Lord and for the benefit of his suffering children. We see that it is Christ himself who is suffering in all the patients. Let me give you a specific example how the spiritual and ethical aspects can be combined. We called a team conference on a child whose heart was stopping every fifteen minutes or so, and they were resuscitating him. The child had spinal bifida and would need a tracheotomy if he were to be kept alive. The doctor knew the child would die anyway. At the start of the conference I read an appropriate scripture passage from the Old Testament. The awareness of the sacred was brought forward immediately at the beginning of our discussion. We were touched by the sacred, and our conversation really became a form of medical prayerful technology.

This kind of process means that we don't stay strictly with the ethical aspects of the case by asking: What is the right thing to do? We bring it to a spiritual level with prayer and scripture. What is the loving thing to do with this child and with these parents? In this way we were all conscious of the presence of God in our midst, and that in the long run we are doing his work among the suffering patients.

XIII

To Comfort and Console

Doctor Samuel is a Jewish neurosurgeon who does brain surgery in both
a proprietary hospital and a public
hospital

*What do you see the chaplains doing at the hospitals where you per-
form operations?*

What they actually do, of course, depends on the personality and style of the individual chaplain, and they are not
all the same. Now, what I would like to see the chaplain do
is to give comfort to a patient and to let the patient ventilate
his anxieties and his feelings, which are usually feelings of
depression. You know that neurosurgery has to do with the
brain area, as opposed, for instance, to the spinal cord. You
know there is no pain at all in the brain; you can do surgery
there without local anesthetic. Cushing did all his great work
digging around in the brain because people can't feel it. But
that doesn't soothe the person who is about to have a brain
operation. As a matter of fact, neurosurgery of the brain is a
very upsetting experience to patients.

It's a new experience for them, and most patients are
frightened half to death beforehand, that is, before the surgery. I am not sure that chaplains ever visit patients in the
hospital for any length of time before the operation. I don't
think the chaplains usually read the medical record. Often-

times the patient, or the patient's family, doesn't inform the chaplain that the person is to go through a series of serious diagnostic tests and is to be operated on. I think the first thing that a chaplain should do for a neurosurgery patient who is in the hospital for a diagnosis and treatment of a brain problem is to counsel the individual, hopefully to comfort him, and especially to let the individual express his feelings.

Why do you think the chaplains don't do this?

I think it's because they don't read the chart. They really do not know what the diagnosis is in most instances. There is an admitting diagnosis, generally on the information sheet in most hospitals today, that would say "suspected brain tumor" or "suspected aneurism." Now, I'm not saying for sure that the chaplains don't read that. But my guess is that most chaplains look at the chart first for the religion of the patient to see which patients they should be visiting. They go in, visit the patients, and ask if there is anything they can do for them. The implication is that the chaplain is a busy man, a little bit too busy to sit down by the bedside and listen to the patient. He is certainly willing to serve the patient, as in the case of the Catholic priest, for some short religious ceremony, confession or a blessing, but he is not really there to give comfort to the patient. At least, that's the impression that I have. The emphasis is not on comforting the patient. Does that make any sense to you?

There is always a real concern when a Catholic patient is about to expire. Even the non-Catholic nurses are very cooperative in calling the priest in to give the last rites. I'm sure that's important to both the patient and his relatives. But I think there is so much more that could be done—and frankly should be done—all the way from the very beginning, before the operation, to comfort the patient and hear him out. In addition to that, when the patient recovers sufficiently to be able to talk a day or two after the surgery, he still has plenty of anxieties. In the immediate post-operative period he doesn't feel much like having a long-winded discussion, but at least he knows that someone is there who is interested in him. Immediately after the operation the patient is frequently not able to communicate for himself, and it's the family then that needs the help. Lastly, when the patient sufficiently recovers he may ask for the diagnosis. When patients ask me flat out "Doctor, was the tumor malignant?" I tell them. I always speak to the family, and am guided by a responsible family member who may want to withhold information from the patient. On the other hand, if the patient himself asks, and if he has his wits about him, then I think he is entitled to know the truth, regardless of what the family says about it.

You know that most of the time the spouse and family need comfort too. Now, once that has happened, I don't think there are any people who can easily handle the news that they have a malignant brain tumor. That is a serious blow to them, and I think it is at that time that the priest, or some other chaplain, could be extremely helpful. One could almost outline a program, but I'm fully aware that this would take an inordinate amount of time to sit down with the patient before surgery, and then sit down with the patient again ten days or two weeks after surgery and hear him out.

You are suggesting that this is not done by the surgeon; it is not done by the nurse or by the social worker. Therefore, it remains the task for the clergyman.

I am not suggesting that it is not done by the physician. At least, I do it, but I can't speak for other physicians. I do it as often and as completely as I can. But basically I'm a stranger in this situation. The individual sees me maybe a few days prior to surgery. The family doesn't know me, and the patient doesn't know me. Even though the chaplain himself may be a stranger too, there is a relationship between a man of the cloth and the patient that is far greater than there is between him and me as an unknown physician.

It's not a question of me substituting for the chaplain, or the chaplain substituting for me. I think there is a very real difference in what I can do because I'm the bad guy, so to speak. I'm the person who is going to do the operation, the one who has to deliver the information concerning the result of the operation—good or bad—and I'm the one who has to tell the patient, if he wants to be told, or the family, that a tumor is malignant. And it's very difficult to play both positions, or to wear two hats, in that regard.

Except that in the newer pastoral-care approach, everyone in the hospital has a holistic concern for the total person.

I wish I thought that was true! Now, my colleagues in medicine frequently, I think, don't voice their compassion for the patient, because many are extremely busy, or many of them because of their personality simply don't get involved with the patient's emotional state, or with the family's emotional needs. The nurses by and large are so busy with paperwork that they don't have time. It's unbelievable what they have to do. When a patient is extremely ill he's generally in the intensive care unit, or the coronary care unit. Those nurses are so busy taking care of the dire medical emergency that they don't have time to comfort the patient in the sense that you and I would think a nurse did in days gone by. Once the patient is transferred out of those units into a ward there are relatively few nurses available.

I am really talking about the licensed practical nurses, as opposed to the regular registered nurse. There are actually three levels, or three echelons. There is usually the R.N. who is the head nurse on a given ward, and she may have one or more R.N.'s helping her. Associated with them are the practical nurses who do more of the bedside nursing, but not a great deal of it. Then there are the nurse's aides. When a patient rings his buzzer, the nurse's aide goes into the room, or perhaps the ward clerk over the intercom system asks the patient what the problem is. Frankly, the patient gets relatively depersonalized in this situation because he doesn't often see a human face. So until the patient rings, other than for the nurse's rounds during the day, or the time when temperature needs to be taken, the patient rarely ever sees a nurse.

The patients see more of the nurse's aides and the nursing assistants than they do of the nurses themselves, who make the rounds perhaps twice during their shift. But they are writing on the chart because everything has to be recorded now—how the patient feels, his temperature. All the tests done for the patient have to be recorded by the nurse. This is part of the defense medicine bit to keep from getting sued for malpractice—I mean the nurse getting sued. Add to that the nursing shortage—and almost every major hospital has a nursing shortage.

Well, let's take them one by one. The doctors, as I said, for one reason or another, don't talk to the patients or their family, or offer comfort, because they don't have enough time, or feel like a stranger, or maybe because of their personality, or whatever. The nurses, as I said, simply don't do it because there are not enough nurses to go around. That leaves only one other person. It's an enormous gap, and to my mind it isn't filled.

So the clergyman is there to take up the slack.

I wouldn't put it quite that way, as though it were just something left over for him to do. He's providing for the compassionate needs of the patient, and you need a lot more than one chaplain in any hospital. They ought to be full-time, and they could be very busy people if they took it seriously and devoted themselves just to the non-medical needs of the patients. In addition—and we have not talked about this—when the patient dies the priest is called for the last rites, and he will generally also want to console the families who need more than just a few words. My secretary is a Catholic and she was in the hospital about two years ago. I told her you were coming in today, and she said that "when the priest chaplain came by to see me in the hospital, I told him I was from St. John's parish. He turned around and walked out of the room, saying that my priest from St. John's would be coming by." Now this lady had a broken hip from an automobile accident. She was in a good bit of pain, was upset emotionally, and could have used something better than that turndown.

What about the hospital chaplains you know personally?

There is one Catholic chaplain I used to see almost every day. He was a very matter-of-fact individual who seemed to give just perfunctory service to the Catholics in the hospital. There were occasional Catholic patients with whom I had more than the usual doctor-patient relationship, and they said that they would really just as soon that he would not even come into their room. But this was an individual matter. For the past three months we have had a priest who is a genuinely nice guy. He is a compassionate soul, very interested in the patients. He sees not only the Catholic patients, but also the non-Catholics who are in a fix. I tell you, if I ever were a patient here I'd be delighted to see him because he is just somebody I could talk to. Often that's all the patients want, and maybe the doctor is not the one they could talk with. What I am really telling you is that there is an enormous vacancy in hospital care as far as the emotional state goes. Whether the priest is the one to fill in that high gap, I don't know, because it would take an inordinate amount of his time.

I think that if somebody had enough time to sit down with a patient and discuss his spiritual state, he would certainly put the patient a great deal more at peace and give him more acceptance. I think this is particularly true from what I know of the Catholic religion. An individual who is deathly ill, or a family that is overwrought, can be put at ease much better by a priest than by a Protestant minister or a rabbi. When patients and their families are in that fix, maybe it's like the saying that "there are no atheists in fox holes." Many people would turn to religion and certainly appreciate some spiritual guidance. Perhaps people don't get that often enough, and I think that lack of time may be the principal problem. It would take at least thirty minutes each time with each patient, and I can see that the chaplain is too busy because he has too many people to see. I guess there's a chaplain shortage just as there is a nurse shortage.

Well, the parish priest is also expected to visit his sick parishioners in the hospital.

We just had an experience with a young man, nineteen years of age, my son's closest friend. The boy had a stroke while water skiing and died five days later. The pastor did a very, very good job. I was at the house when he gave a short ceremony and later at the funeral parlor when he had another service. He said some very nice things about the boy and tried to make it easy for the family, to explain how God could take a nineteen year old otherwise healthy young man. Then he had a very nice Mass at the parish church for the funeral service. This is the kind of spiritual help that people need. Whatever spirituality he invokes to do this is immaterial to me. Just because he's Catholic and I'm Jewish doesn't mean that I don't understand. I understand fully what he is doing, and I applaud him for having done it. This helped that family immeasurably, and I can't imagine it being done by a hospital chaplain because of the very time element.

One of the interesting developments is that women religious are being trained for pastoral care in hospitals.

I have the feeling that someone would not be as willing to talk to a nun as to a priest. Maybe I'm mistaken about that, but in this office we have four Catholic women working for us. Their reaction—those who went to parochial schools—was that they would really not want to deal with a nun, because the nun is an authoritarian figure, a symbol of discipline to them, whereas the priest was always the father image to whom they could talk. I found this an interesting difference.

Well, this is simply an impression that I have. I think it would take a real change in the public's attitude to accept female ministers, priests, or clergy of any kind. The women's lib bit has to go into this too, of course. There are about eighty women rabbis in the country; there's even one here in the city. I keep hearing about the attempts to ordain women priests in the Catholic Church. I think it would take some kind of public relations effort on the part of the hospital, as well as on the part of the Catholic Church, to inform lay Catholics that the hospital chaplains are now nuns. It occurs to me that the hospital should have some responsibility here in making it known that sisters have been trained in hospital pastoral care. As you probably know, when you enter the hospital as a patient you are handed a brochure which is a kind of pep talk saying how great we are and what we do for you. It appeals to the emotions, and somewhat to the soul of the patient, as well as to his body. I just wonder whether it would be advisable to say in the brochure that there are trained specialists in pastoral care. "If he or she does not appear during the first day or two of your hospitalization, would you please let us know and we will see to it that he or she comes."

So you put that responsibility on the hospital administration?

I think the administration should inform the patients that this kind of service is available. Patients begin to get religion, so to speak, when they are in danger of their lives, more so than when they are not. I think they are entitled to such care. This is not asking too much of a hospital administration, and I would think that most of them would be pleased to cooperate, and particularly the Catholic hospitals. I would think that the sister-in-charge would be delighted to go along with that.

I understand that the church-related hospitals support financially their own chaplains. Certainly the Catholic Church sees to it that their priests visit the sick regularly. Many other churches expect the local ministers to visit the sick members of the congregation. I know two Protestant ministers who for one reason or another were eased out of their congregations and were given the job of hospital chaplain. For them it was like being sent to Alaska if you are in the army. I can't imagine that either of these gentlemen thought highly of the task they were assigned, or knew much about it. Obviously, it would have been different if they were trained for this kind of job. Let me add that most hospitals that have been built recently, or have had additions rebuilt, have non-denominational chapels, but they are used virtually not at all in the hospitals I know. Of course, the Catholic hospitals make use of their chapels for regular services, like the Mass for ambulatory patients and staff. But, by and large, I think the kind of spiritual care we have been talking about has been neglected.

We hear a lot these days about the holistic concept that focuses all the hospital personnel onto each patient. That's true and it's good but, again theoretically, everyone should be concerned with the patient, from the doctor to the resident staff at the hospital, to the head nurse and her nursing assistants; all should have some interest in this, but from a practical standpoint that just isn't going to happen. You can't make people do something they're not accustomed to doing. I think people basically are compassionate and caring individuals, or they are not.

Well, can't they be trained? For example, when you went through medical school was there ever any mention of this?

Absolutely not. There was no mention of this by anybody whatever. The patient as a whole human being, that is to say, his emotional state in addition to his physical state, was not mentioned, not even in the psychiatry teaching. And I doubt seriously that there is much emphasis on this now. Frankly, most of the younger doctors today, I think, would laugh at this. This gets back, I believe, to a concept that people had fifty years ago about the family doctor or general practitioner, where they thought you really had to take care of the whole individual. Today, medicine is so compartmentalized really that I take care of the nervous system, somebody else takes care of the bones, somebody else takes care of the heart, and so forth.

Now it is still true, outside of the hospital routine, that many people generally have a pretty decent relationship with their regular physician. In a sense, it is the general practitioner to whom they will go if they have a problem. That doctor is usually an internist, who is harried and worn, and has entirely too many patients. Although the patient often feels that he wants to talk to the doctor, the doctor is not willing to listen to anything other than the physical complaints. And that's also a matter of time. Then when the doctor calls in a consultant, such as myself, the consultant focuses on one aspect. He doesn't know anything about the patient's background, and when that one aspect is dealt with, he steps out. So, although I understand the problem, I think the solution to the problem is a very difficult one if we are looking to the physician to add anything.

I guess I ought to try to summarize to see if we are in contact with each other. It boils down to a religiously trained individual who has a sufficient amount of time to be able to discuss with the patient from the first or second day he's in the hospital to the time that he recovers, as well as with the family during the time of great stress. The basic compassionate and emotional needs on the lower level should be met by everybody, and the spiritual comfort on the higher level is offered mainly by the clergyman. Theoretically, this sounds fine, but from a practical standpoint you are still faced with many problems. One is the ratio of priest to patients; a second is the individual character of the priest as a human being, and his training and background; a third is the simple limitation of time that the chaplain has to perform his job. Holistic healing can't be rushed.

XIV

Suffering Can Be Awesome

Reverend Sylvia, an ordained Lutheran minister, is director of chaplaincy at a 600-bed nondenomina-
tional teaching hospital

Is professional pastoral care different in Canada?

Perhaps only in accreditation and career preparation. I
have the master of divinity degree from the Lutheran seminary and was ordained to the clergy. I have two years of advanced clinical pastoral education: four units in CPE and a
year of internship at the University Medical Center. In Canada we have what is called certification for a specialist in institutional ministry, and I have the specialty in hospital
chaplaincy. It's a new certification program that recognizes
the need for people who have some competency within institutional chaplaincy. Previously, the clinical training movement was focused primarily on training supervisors in
pastoral education. The current program is run by a separate
organization made up of people who had clinical training
themselves, most of whom are ordained in various churches.

It is almost in the model of apprenticeship, or even a physician's year of residency. You learn by doing and by reflect-
ing upon that experience under supervision. The majority of
the time is actually spent ministering to patients and their
families. You have a lot of time to be exposed to the whole

health care system, the various medical disciplines, to gain some familiarity with different disease processes and treatments. Then a lot of time is spent in supervision to look at how you are functioning in those relationships. You reflect pastorally and theologically upon these experiences.

The academic content of the pastoral care training for hospital chaplaincy is both theological and psychological. The attention paid to the theological isn't so much a didactic content, like presenting systematic theology or any new and different doctrine. The teaching helps you to find ways to distill the religious meaning of people's experience who are confronting a crisis of illness and suffering in their life. It's more experientially oriented than academic, such as: "What does this real life experience say to us about our relationship with God and with others? What is the purpose of our life? What do we value or hold dear? What values we may need to let go of at this time in our life." So, the theological reflection is not about any particular dogmatic theological systems.

How do you handle the religious content when dealing with patients?

I function as a chaplain hired by the hospital, sensitive to the wants and needs of the patient, answering any questions they have, and aware that this is a voluntary relationship of ministry with the patient. This is voluntary for the patient because it differs from the almost compulsory relationship imposed by the medical personnel, like nurses and doctors. The religious content is delicate because there are some people who do not welcome a representative of the church, and they may have various reasons for this. There may have been a very negative experience in their history. It may be that they don't want a priest or rabbi to know they are in the hospital for a particular procedure or illness. It may be a variety of reasons. Perhaps they expect that someone visiting them in the hospital, from a church or a synagogue, will simply come in and say a prayer or read a portion of the scripture and then leave, and they don't want that. Their expectation may not fit the reality of what's being offered by the chaplains. I think we need to respect people's wishes. In fact, legally we are bound to do so.

I am the director of chaplaincy, and we have about twelve denominational chaplains who visit the sick for various lengths of time. They need direction in handling the religious content of their ministry. They are not there full-time. They also have other assignments, such as in a local congregation, and they are responsible to their various church bodies. They are responsible to me and to the administration in the sense that they are accountable for the various hospital procedures and policies in their visiting. I help to facilitate their ministry, give them access to patients when that's appropriate, and make that easier for them. Because they are part-time most of them have not had specific training for hospital work. I try to give them some comfort in the hospital setting when they feel out of place and don't really know how to offer their ministry to the best advantage of the sick patients.

We do not have a pastoral care training center here, but we are working toward that. I love teaching, and I do a lot of training for lay pastoral visitors who work with the chaplains. And I do some training with students on field placement from the seminaries in town. But the title of "teaching hospital" refers strictly to the teaching of interns and medical students who are doing their residency there. The hospital is also a referral center for cases from other hospitals, which means that most of the patients have a serious disease or are acutely ill. Of course, there is an intensive care unit, but also a specialty in rheumatic diseases, and we have a new burn center. Our chaplains also have to take care of the hospital next door, which has 200 active treatment beds with a very large outpatient treatment center. There is also a lodge on the premises that accommodates 100 out-of-town patients who are up and about but who are receiving treatment.

How do you relate in general to the staff?

Well, it takes a while to educate the hospital staff when they have gotten themselves into a real bind, such as when they're having difficulty with the family of a dying patient, or with a patient who just got bad news from the doctor. They will phone me in an emergency, but they often have trouble realizing that the involvement of the chaplain would be important earlier on. The chaplains often get called when no one else is available, or when no one else knows what to do. For my direct patient care and ministry to families I'm usually responding to requests from head nurses, sometimes from doctors, or it may even be self-referral of one of the patients.

When the social workers and the psychiatrists, and the other support services, haven't been able to deal with a problem, then they'll call the chaplain. But I find that in my hospital there is a growing awareness of the importance of seriously considering the spiritual needs of patients in relation to their physical and emotional health. I even hate using those labels because the more time I spend with patients, and hear their stories, the more aware I become of how integral a spiritual, emotional, physical human being is. When you ask me how I minister to the spiritual needs of a patient, I just can't answer that because I don't see the spiritual in isolation from what's happening to them physically and emotionally.

They are trained to do their own thing, but a lot of my job is also affirming the kind of spiritual and emotional support that the nursing staff are able to give, and do give, and to provide them some encouragement in that. Also, the physicians and all the health care workers sometimes come in on a consultation. They'll say, "We have this problem, or this concern, with this patient or the family." Then we'll spend some time with the staff examining it. What we discover usually is that someone is ministering very well to this person's needs but just needs a little help and support to identify the issues more clearly and how he might do that better. I never get directly involved with patients when I see someone is already speaking to those needs. It doesn't necessarily have to be an ordained person to respond to their spiritual needs.

Critics say that health care has become so technical that the patient's relationship with God is ignored.

I think there is a growing sensitivity to the religious factor, which is partly because the whole discipline of chaplains within hospitals has been evolving over the last several years. I think we have had a hard job of identifying our functions, our roles, what kind of skills we bring, and also the importance of realizing how this expression of illness is very related to the spiritual health and well-being of the individuals we work with. Now, I work non-denominationally; I may be called in to see someone who has really no connection with any religious community, or else to see people who have a very deep involvement within their religious community. So the language that I use to speak about their spiritual journey will be quite different, given the person. Yet I find that the questions that they raise, or the points where they're hurting and they're suffering, their hopes and dreams, are not that different, given their experience. Symbolically, I am identified as a chaplain, and people do recognize what that means. I am there because I am part of a religious community.

Do you wear a white coat like the nurse and the doctor?

No, I don't. I wear regular street clothes. I don't wear a white coat because often the chaplains and I are the only ones who enter the patient's room during the day who do not have a lab coat on. Because of that people are more free to engage in conversation in a different way than if you wear any religious identification, except maybe the name tag that says you're a chaplain. The reason for this is because any religious identification I may choose to wear is not a universal symbol, and I relate to Jewish people, Hindus, Pentecostals, and others. I don't wear the Christian cross, but I tell them who I am. I think there are ways of doing that without wearing some religious badge or identification. I am quite willing to share that with them, and I do. But I'm there to support them in their journey of faith, and that will be different if I'm talking

to someone from the Jewish community or from the Roman
Catholic community.

Do you get resistance from patients who don't want to see a pastor,
especially a woman pastor?

Somehow I have a way of presenting myself that they accept me. Usually my patients are so hungry for human dialogue around these important issues in their lives that if you
can give them a glimpse of why you are there they very early
welcome that relationship. I've been doing this now for six
years, and I can only remember three times where the resistance was so obvious or they quite frankly said, "No, I'm not
interested." Now, about being a clergywoman. It is still a bit
unusual to have women as hospital chaplains just because
there are so few of us ordained within the Christian church
in the first place. It was a little bit of a problem when I went
through the search committee. But there are very strong leaders within our hospital, who are women. The executive director happens to be a woman.

My relationship with the doctors is still uneven. I have
confronted a little hostility. It's usually that they really don't
know what you are about, or what you are there for. Often,
because I do know what people are experiencing in their illness and in their treatments, I become an advocate for patients when they are having difficulty in communicating with
their physician. But I am pretty straight about confronting
them when I think that their treatment or their relationship
with the patient is doing violence to the person or is not respectful of the patient's struggle with spiritual values.

Are there instances of physicians who neglect this?

For example, take a patient who has had a long chronic
illness and then suffered some kind of crisis like a stroke and
is now on extreme life supports, like ventilators. If I know
that this patient has expressed his feelings about death, perhaps his faith around the hope for life after death, I let this be
known. If I find that the physicians are not aware of this, or

are not respecting it, or have avoided being with the family, I'll call them on that. I have the support of the administration if that doesn't follow through. I have a lot of power in a critical situation like that.

As a matter of fact, I have to spend a lot of time, in a teaching hospital like ours, with the residents in training. Even at that point in their career they have had little experience dealing in a human way with patients and their families. So when it comes time to get autopsy requests, to share bad news, to try to get a decision or a consent from a family, or when it comes time for sharing the news of death with the grieving family, I spend a lot of time modeling behavior for the young residents. I don't take that responsibility from them, or do it for them, as some chaplains do—they'll call the family and inform them that there has been a death. I think that's the responsibility of the physician, and I insist on it. The family has the right to know the relevant medical facts around what happened, and they really trust that only when it comes from the physician. I can tell them the same thing; the nurse can tell them the same thing; they still want to see the doctor and to know if everything that could have been done was done.

This teaching seems to be postponed until their year of residency in a teaching hospital and then, almost by default, it becomes the task of the chaplain to model this behavior for them. This part of my work then is perhaps not overtly religious. Does the chaplaincy then turn into social work, or does it get overpsychologized? I think it is the chaplain's prerogative to model human behavior that respects the human spirit and the kind of impact on people's lives that is made by the facts of pain and death. You also have to model how you are able to be there with people, help them confront the truth in their lives, and give them support without becoming over-paternalistic and making decisions for them.

Does this kind of work affect you emotionally? Do you cry?

You'd have to be pretty wooden not to cry sometimes. You know, you might expect that somehow it would get easier over the years. Instead, it gets harder, because as I learn more and am able to open myself more to other people's lives and their searches, their hopes, their fears, I become more vulnerable to that. I also become more aware of how their experience touches on my own questions, my own suffering, my own grief. There are times when I get a phone call from one of the head nurses who tells me about a patient who has become what she calls "difficult"; then I feel like hitting the office wall with my fist because we have all sorts of ways to try to lay meaning on these kinds of events. I think the tragedy in them is that maybe ultimately there isn't meaning in the event itself but only in our response to it.

Sometimes you feel drained and empty. What keeps me there, though, is the awesomeness of what you see happening in people's lives in the midst of their suffering. Sometimes it's just plain violent awesomeness that doesn't seem to be connected objectively in any way with the actual physical pain—if you can measure that—or the circumstances of the story. It is in that person's response to what is happening to them. Maybe in their whole life this is just one more event they can't handle. It is one more time when their own personal, spiritual, and emotional resources fail them. The resources of the family, the network of community and people around them, have been so void that there seems little possibility of redeeming anything out of this tragedy. But then others may face the same tragic challenge differently because in their own life story they have experienced love and care and compassion and God.

My assumption is that a religious person can handle tragedy more readily.

Certainly you encounter people who face a crisis in their life, their own chronic illness, the death of a spouse, with inner peace, and I imagine they are a kind of magic people. Our faith does not prevent the hurt and the pain, and does not protect us from them. There are some very deeply religious people who are part of the community of faith, very mature spiritually, and yet they experience deep agony and suffering. They may come up with a new understanding of faith and with a better relationship to God, but a person's religious history and experience do not necessarily separate those who have a gentler time of it from those who don't.

Do nurses do better than doctors in the spiritual aspects of health care?

You can't make generalizations, but I'll make one anyway. The nurses always have more immediate patient contact than the doctors. Now some are still quite able to go in and check the I.V. fluid and just leave the room. The only thing they relate to is that I.V. call. That's sad to see and is readily recognized by the patient when that happens. But I think that most nurses have more personal contact with the patient over extended periods of time, not only in the medical chores, but also physically with bathing and feeding, and that's where the practical nurse is present. Because of that physical closeness there develops a good human dialogue between patient and the nursing staff. This seldom happens with physicians or social workers. Because of that the nurses are very much aware of the spiritual dimensions and the religious needs of people. Because patients are ready to articulate that to the nursing staff, the nurses sometimes feel uncomfortable trying to respond to it. They say, "This is getting into theological issues," or "I don't know enough about religion to say anything worthwhile."

That's what the nurses tell me, and often I'll try to help them feel more comfortable and free in responding to that simply as another human person who shares that quest, who shares that aspect of living without proselytizing. They should simply recognize that this is a common part of our human existence, and this does give spiritual support to the patient. Now that means that the nurse also needs to be alert when patients are asking to see a representative of their faith, or have sacramental needs, or specific needs like being hungry for a scripture reading. Perhaps underneath what they are really asking for is the opportunity to confess to a minister of their church. Actually, I get most of my referrals from the nursing staff.

Do the nurses need your support too, or are they pretty tough people?

The toughest ones usually run into problems because you can maintain that stance only for so long and have your job be fulfilling for you. Most health care professionals, including physicians, have a motivation for going into it that reflects compassion and the desire to spend their life energy in a certain way, caring for others. Then after their studies they find themselves all of a sudden in the real world with a lot of machinery around them and the demands of their job that won't allow time for caring. And they experience a violence professionally and personally because of that.

You'll often find that those who harden themselves to the pain and suffering around them don't last long in the practice of immediate health care. But if you open yourself to that hurt, if you recognize your loss when a patient dies, you need some human support, and that becomes mutual. When I'm working with a patient and I see a couple of nurses pretty deeply involved with this patient or this family, I'll make it a point of seeking them out when they are having a tough time, or after the patient dies. Sometimes it's simply having coffee together, quietly talking about what that experience can mean for us. Sometimes it's crying together. And sometimes it's praying together. At other times, and more in general, I do in-service teaching to make the nursing staff aware of the spiritual needs of patients but also their own personal and professional needs. I ask them to share their own experiences so they can sift out what is sustaining and fulfilling, and also what they find devastating in their work and relationships.

XV

Caring Is Healing

Father Kevin is the Jesuit director of
pastoral care training in a 400-bed
Catholic hospital of a university medical school

Older hospital chaplains complain that CPE training is turning cler-
gymen into psychiatrists.

The switch from the old-line quick-visit sacramental type
of chaplaincy has produced such a different concept of hospital ministry that the old-timers are a little confused by it. But
there is also some basis for that complaint from students who
trained under over-zealous supervisors. It is true that the
training program accredited by the Association for Clinical
Pastoral Education tends to be heavily psychological. What I
am directing here at this Catholic hospital is a training program that fits the standards of the National Association of
Catholic Chaplains. We are an accredited program for training pastoral care personnel. Our curriculum had to be reviewed and approved by the Association, and, through
them, by the bishops of the United States.

The tendency of some Catholic critics is to specify the
CPE as a "Protestant" organization, but I want to assure you
that some of its approved supervisors are Catholic priests and
sisters; it is accredited in some Catholic hospitals, and provides training for the students of some Catholic seminaries.

It is a fact, however, that the content of its teaching and training avoids theological positions or even statements that have to do with what we ordinarily call religious beliefs. You said in your own book on *Religion and Pain* that their approach is more clinical than pastoral. It is heavy on counseling and psychology that put the patient at ease at a natural and this-worldly level.

Yet I did have reports from sisters and seminarians who were not allowed to wear clerical garb, or even a medal or cross, to identify themselves as pastoral ministers.

These are probably exceptional cases of rules made by supervisors who overemphasize the avoidance of what they call ecclesiastical intervention. Other supervisors in other schools are not nearly that extreme. The point they make is that they want to reach the patient at the patient's emotional level, to meet the needs of the patient rather than to fulfill the expectations of the clerical or religious role. In other words, you must not intrude. You must find out first what the sick person's needs are before you start offering him God, or religion, or the church. In all charity, I think I can say that the Protestant pastors have two inherent drawbacks. The first is that they do not have a well-developed sacramental system which has been the traditional Christian source of supernatural grace. Secondly, even when they read the scriptures for the consolation or guidance of the patient they may have wide differences of interpretation of the Bible. I myself did two units of the ACPE training, and I think my general interpretation is pretty fair. I was not really satisfied with it, but I am sure that their training is done better in some places than in others.

First of all, we have a more structured academic program than ACPE. We screen the students very carefully, so that we do not have to take time to free them from their own emotional and psychological hang-ups. Our trainees have to be intellectually competent as well as emotionally stable. So the morning is spent in the classroom and the afternoon on the hospital wards. There may be a lecture on ministry through

the sacraments, or on becoming a person, or on the psychological aspects of dealing with hospitalized persons. We will
have a filmstrip on guidelines for the dying person, followed
by questions and a discussion. The students also have to do
two seminars in which they are assigned a subject and given
three or four weeks to prepare it. This means they have to do
research in the field of health care, report to the group, and
be prepared to explain the topic. In other words, we pursue
an academic curriculum that was constructed on the basis of
our hospital pastoral experiences.

*How is religion brought to the ordinary hospital patient? Is the chap-
lain the only one who does this?*

I don't think so. We believe that every person in this hospital brings religion to the suffering patient, and brings it essentially in the form of personal caring. Whether they are in
the dietary department or the maintenance crew, or are
nurse's aides or orderlies, they are all focused directly or indirectly on patient care. This we believe is the heart of our
work. When a person knows he is cared for, God comes into
the picture, and healing is more likely to take place. Caring is
closely linked to healing.

For a believer on the medical staff, caring for the sick is
the Christian virtue of love. Certainly a secular humanist or
agnostic could demonstrate human love for others, but I
think the Christian approach provides a little more depth and
insight. Obviously, for the Christian, we see the tremendous
value of the redemptive suffering of Jesus, and we have to try
to get this across to sick people, as a solace if not as an explanation of their pain.

I guess it gets across in many ways because everybody is
different from everybody else. One of the points we teach our
students is this: always take the patient where he is, not
where you want him to be. Most trainees tend to be too
tightly bound at first; they know only one way to pray and
they want to use it right away, or they come in and start reading the Bible. The experience that we have had is that most
people who are really hurting are so concerned with their

pain that they don't have much time for the spiritual. When you have a terrible ache in your body, or in your head, it's pretty tough to think of something else. You must first be alert to their need and see if you can be helpful. Maybe they can't reach the water; maybe they've been trying to get the nurse and you can help them. You are showing that you care, that you are willing to listen to them. At times I think you can't do anything more than that. As I say, it depends where the person is, and you may be able to tell him about the suffering Christ, or the wounded Christ. It may be, if you have a listener there in the bed, that all aspects of Jesus' life can be brought to bear.

While you are doing all this, is it your function to get the patient's mind off his pain? Do you alleviate his hurt?

No, I don't think so. I don't think you can. What they really want is someone to hear their moans and groans, and criticisms. This is why you have to listen before you speak. They have something to say, and they want somebody to hear them rather than someone to come in and try to tell them. That's why I strongly believe in having a crucifix on the wall of the patient's room. The symbol is there that the Lord has suffered with them and for them. Many patients—not all of them—have told me that "it is a great inspiration and consolation."

Everybody on the staff, everybody in this hospital, has a share in pastoral care, at least to make people comfortable and spiritually at ease. The least you can say, I suppose, is that it is indirectly pastoral. The social worker, or the nurse, or anybody else, is able to do this, but we know that they don't. Each of them has a professional job to do specifically, and they don't have time. But our job is first just to have time for the patient. We are not, and should not be, in a hurry. Secondly, we come on as a living witness of something more than physical medical care. I feel that in my own life of faith I am a living witness to the Gospel, and that the patients know this.

Do the nuns on your pastoral team wear the religious habit?

No, they wear ordinary street garb, and they admit that it is sometimes difficult for them to establish their identity as sisters. The same thing happened this last quarter, with a layman who had to identify himself as a pastoral care person. But once the patients saw that he cared and that he had time to give them, he was in and the nurses began referring patients to him. The biggest thing of all is the presence of a caring person who witnesses to God and faith, and that's true of the Protestant minister too. I think in the Catholic hospital the collar is terribly advantageous, but I have seen Protestant clergy in their coat and tie ministering effectively. However, I have also seen them come on too strong with the spiritual pitch, and so they minister ineffectively.

What is the secret to effective pastoral ministry?

The patient has to be ready for you. What you are driving at, what you are looking for, is very tenuous. The presence of the chaplain in the sick room means a great deal, whether it is sacramental or scriptural, or just being a human being as they are. A lot of people are sick today because nobody cares about them. That's an important factor in sickness. I work on the psych ward, and that's a big element with those patients. As soon as you show some interest in them, and they recognize that you stand for something, you can lead them into a more spiritual type of setting.

Sometimes people will ask, "Father, would you say a prayer?" If they are older, you just say an Our Father or a Hail Mary because that's what they know best and expect. If they are younger, I use a contemporary prayer. So that's if they ask for prayer. Secondly, you have situations that are full of stress, such as in the emergency room with a stabbing, or an accident, or a cardiac arrest. Then the human element has to be cleared away, and they regain consciousness and are able to talk. Often they are scared, and they begin to talk to you as a priest. But I have a sensitivity to their need because they may not need prayer just then. They are so caught up in the human element. I want to get away from the old-fashioned formula that says: "I did what I was supposed to do. I said a prayer and took care of that. So we are all right now." But that isn't really always enough. As an example, in one incident when I pushed to do more than a prayer, I found a large scene of deep human anguish. This was the sixth member of the family in the hospital this year. Five had died. Then all of a sudden it all starts to come out why these people are so distracted.

Is the need for contact with the patient's family and relatives something new in pastoral care training?

I think it's fairly new for the Catholic chaplains. This again is where the Protestants were way ahead of us. They took the time to do the counseling and saw the total picture, and the inference we made is that they don't have a multitude of people to take care of what the parish priest has. In the Catholic hospital the sacramental thing was to go in and anoint the dying person and leave the room. The priest had done his duty, and he also had to say Mass for the hospital nuns.

At the present time all the pastoral care supervisors say: Move toward the relatives, help comfort them, help them to work through their grief and their guilt patterns, of whatever nature they may be. The most important aspect, the one I find most successful, is to help them see God's blessings in their lives. They get some understanding of their tragedy. They overcome their sorrow and their guilt. They begin to recall the good times of their lives, and that they have had many experiences to be thankful for. It is not easy to do this with them; it requires tact and patience, and close attention. This is different from the routine of a quick prayer and a sacrament, and priests need training for it. I think there isn't a pastoral training school today that bypasses the relatives of the sick and dying.

*The reputation of the big-city hospital chaplain was that he was over-
burdened with work, always on call to the emergency room, to hear
somebody's confession, to bring Communion to every Catholic in the
morning.*

That's the situation we are trying to correct, and we have
to apply a double remedy: we simply have to have more people on the pastoral team, religious men and women, laymen
and women, and, secondly, they have to be trained on how
to deal with both patients and their family, and also with all
the hospital personnel. Fortunately, here in this hospital we
have eight people working in pastoral ministry; we have a
team of five fully trained persons, and then we get in three
students each quarter. All comments from the students who
write their critique of the program say that they like to have
three to four hours in the afternoon around the wards. They
are getting the practical aspects of pastoral care under supervision, and right there on the floor.

You have to have enough people to do the job right. The
ratio recommended by the National Association of Catholic
Chaplains is one for every fifty beds. So, if you have a 400-
bed hospital, like this one, you need eight chaplains, and
that's what we have, including students in training. There's
a certain degree of stress you naturally feel in this kind of
ministry. You can't take care of sick people day in and day
out without losing your sense of reality and your real appreciation for life. You have to have time to recharge your bat-
teries, have time for yourself and for your own personal
growth. My strong convictions about this come out of some
unhappy experiences.

After I completed my training program, four units of
Clinical Pastoral Education at a fine Lutheran hospital, I
shifted to one of the largest Catholic hospitals in the country,
with a capacity of over 1,500 beds, and we were dreadfully
understaffed. A couple of older priests did their work in the
traditional way, and we had two religious women who were
called pastoral associates, but had not gone through the training. That left only three of us priests who had come out of
accredited pastoral care education. The demands of the job

were really much more than you could reasonably do. During the six years I spent there I saw chaplains come and go. They were very devoted, but they were lasting only two or three years before they burned out and had to go back to parish work. Before I came here I asked for several months off to travel around the country and visit pastoral care departments at all kinds of hospitals. The result was that I knew what I needed here; I got a free hand to build a good program with good people, and I think we are doing all right.

Is there some way of measuring the success of a pastoral care program in bringing religion to suffering people?

Probably not with the techniques a sociologist wants to apply. I don't think you could provide the kind of caring we try to do, unless you have the doctrine and the faith, and I presuppose that. I guess the problem isn't completely clear in anybody's mind. All I know is that many people, when they are able to talk again after their worst pain of an operation or a sickness, make comments like "Thanks for being here" or "Thanks for coming in and staying with me." You helped a little bit, but certainly you didn't eliminate the pain. But there's a whole range of cases, and some are tougher than others. If you have a paraplegic who will be on a long-range program, you have to bring in a heavier doctrine to understand suffering. We have to realize that in the initial stages, the first six weeks or so, the human element is enormous. All of us have to have this in mind as we work through the suffering. You want to console the patient and you tell him, "Well, say your rosary," but that takes concentration. You say to them, "Read a prayer out of your prayer book," but they can't do it; the concentration is gone, the mind is weak, the hands are feeble. They just don't have the energy.

In general, I'm very pleased with the work our pastoral team does. Many of the patients appreciate them. Time and again we get reports that people say, "It was just great having you." We bring a stabilizing influence of the faith to a lot of people, but I guess it's hard to describe and impossible to measure.

*Do you have people like the charismatics come in and lay hands on
the sick?*

No, we don't have much of that at this hospital. A couple
months ago I did participate with a Presbyterian minister in
a case where there was a laying on of hands. The ceremony
was very much like our sacrament of the sick. I think some of
the pentecostal people are doing that sort of thing, but it's not
big here among our Catholics. I should emphasize though
that touching the patients has a great significance in showing
that we care for them—holding their hands, touching them
on the shoulder. We say a blessing while holding a hand on
their head. That's very beneficial for them.

Of course, the medical people can point out that drugs
are a more dependable pain relief than the laying on of hands.
From the evidence I will have to agree with that. Nowadays,
when you walk down a hospital corridor you don't hear patients groaning and moaning the way they used to. Treatment procedures are so improved that when people are really
hurting they are dosed with drugs. I just underwent surgery
last year, and for two days I was completely out. I didn't
know from nothing. The third day I came to, and the healing
was already taking place. This is a tremendous modern improvement. When the healing begins to take place after an
operation, the drugs are gradually replaced so that people
don't experience all this pain that we sometimes think they
do.

XVI

From Home Care to Hospice

Medical social worker Gladys is coordinator of the hospice program at a
large non-denominational medical
center

*What experience do you bring in preparation for your current posi-
tion in this hospital?*

I have a master's degree in medical social work from a big
Jesuit university. Ever since I came to this hospital I've been
teaching sociology at our local community college, especially
social problems of health. I was working for ten years in the
center's home health program before starting up the hospice
department. One thing led to another; the hospice plan grew
out of the home care system, which served as a practical kind
of on-the-job training for me to move right into hospice work.
I used to be a member of a religious order of hospital sisters
and, of course, I consider this ministry to the dying and the
bereaved as a continuation of my spiritual vocation.

Give me a bit of the local history of hospice.

If we go back far enough, the home health care program
grew out of a predecessor: an independent visiting nurses

153

service that started here in the mid-1950's. They limited themselves strictly to home health aid service. Later on, when I first got here, the hospital administration decided to extend its therapy services to patients who had been discharged from the hospital, and also to so-called outpatients who did not need complete hospital care. The philosophy behind this move is that patients could recuperate better and less expensively in their familiar home surroundings, and as a practical matter it meant that more hospital beds were available for people who really needed them.

The visiting nurses service was well organized, and I'm sure they made a good contribution to the health of people who could afford their services, but in a sense they enjoyed a sort of monopoly here. Their executive committee refused to expand for the inclusion of needed ancillary services, like physical therapy, speech therapy, and the occupational therapies. I suppose they thought of themselves as professional specialists and did not want to take on any ancillary services. Theirs was the only home care health program in the community, and they had no fear of competition.

At any rate, the way things worked out in this community, you can visualize a continuity, a connecting relationship, in the care of patients that runs from hospital to visiting nurses, to home care, to hospice, even though it did not develop quite so smoothly and logically. If you start back with the chaplain's pastoral care in the hospital you recall that the chaplain was often summoned to minister to the patient after a serious operation, and to the patient's family who worried about that operation or serious illness, and was also in need of consolation and comforting when a death occurs. In other words, the follow-up of the patient and his family was spiritual as well as medical. In the ordinary course of events these two functions were performed by the person's home pastor, or minister, and by the regular personal or family physician. This tended to be individualistic and unorganized, so that many ex-patients and their families were not receiving the kind of after-care they needed.

Was the home care system replaced by the hospice program?

No, I didn't mean to give you that impression. One can say that the hospice evolved from a combination of pastoral care and home care, but the home care procedures are popular and successful. I am no longer directly connected with home care. It is a separate department with almost fifty employees, all of whom deal only with out-patients who are home-bound. In a real sense, we want to keep people out of the hospital as much as possible, and the hospital administration fully approves of this principle of operation. On a daily basis our census is around 350 patients, and we make approximately two thousand home visits a month. We have nurses, social workers, therapists, a psychologist, and several part-time chaplains. The referrals are made by the discharge nurse and sometimes by the hospital chaplains; less often a family member may make a request; but we will not even discuss home care with a person or make a home visit without the approval of the individual's physician.

There is one other service, the homemaker program, that I wish we could expand. We have separate funding for that, but we can supply only four homemakers who do not live full-time in the patient's home, which is a very expensive service. The homemaker provides what is called a "chore service," administered by our home health care department but funded by the State Commission on Aging. Patients who are over sixty years of age, live in this county and with low-fixed income insufficient to pay for the service can receive help with personal care, light housekeeping, occasional transportation for shopping and to the doctor's office. Unfortunately, this aspect of our program is minimal, but fortunately, in every part of the county, we were able to find volunteer church groups, mainly women who are willing to take up much of this chore service.

How does the hospice differ from home health care?

I guess it is a special type of home care. Hospice care is designed to meet the physical and emotional needs of people

with life-threatening disease, as well as the needs of their
family who care for them. I don't know if you are aware of
the federal government's interest in the hospice. The old Department of Health, Education and Welfare financed twenty-
six demonstration programs around the country to explore
hospice, and we were one of the recipients of the grant. I was
asked by the hospital administration to get the hospice program under way. The government grant gave us a real boost.
It waived all the Medicare and Medicaid restrictions, such as
the home-bound requirement and some of the paperwork requirements. It paid for medication, for some equipment, for
psychology back-up, and that sort of thing.

The government came late to hospice support, didn't it?

Oh yes. But the medical, psychological and spiritual concern over bereavement and grief counseling has a long history. Fulton's bibliography on *Death, Grief and Bereavement* has
over 9,000 entries in the English language alone. That doesn't
mean that the developed concept of the hospice has been
around for a long time. In this country the greatest impetus
for hospice came from Kübler-Ross' book on *Death and Dying*,
and the publicity she got on her five stages of dying. She has
lost some of her influence by this time, but when she was in
vogue practically everybody was quoting her. I suppose it
was St. Christopher Hospice in England that caught the popular imagination and became a kind of exemplar for us in
America. I would say that ninety percent of the hospice programs in this country started as home care of seriously ill patients.

The central concept of hospice, that we focus on the family of the patient and not the patient alone, is nothing new.
Our nurses in home care always made bereavement visits.
They would be free to go to funerals if they wanted to. But
the notion of concentrating all these patients under the care
of one team, and then providing twenty-four hour service—
that was new to us. That is the full hospice, when you have
the team approach and you usually have a joint visit of the
nurse and the social worker to the home of the patient. We

have a medical director for that program, psychological counseling, and, of course, always the spiritual ministry of the
clergyman. In one sense that is the heart of the program and,
as I read somewhere, "the management of loss and grief has
been one of the main concerns of the rituals of religion."

*Well, maybe, but the funeral dirge has been replaced by the Alleluias
in the Mass of the Resurrection.*

That's good. Let me back up to the living person who is
terminally ill, around whom the hospice idea started. Patients
referred to us have a life expectancy between six weeks and
six months. It is very hard for a doctor to tell us exactly how
long a patient still has. Some have lived longer; we have even
discharged some patients who have gotten better and no
longer needed us. Also, we've had some who lived a very
brief period of time. In either case, we usually stay involved
with the family. If they need us we'll be here.

*What is a typical situation? Does the chaplain alert you to the seri-
ously sick person?*

Yes, that's most often the case with a patient in the hospital here. But anybody could make the referral. You could
tell me that you know somebody, a neighbor, friend or relative who would benefit from our program. You could call up
and tell us something about the patient. I then call the patient's doctor, just to make sure he knows we are involved,
and also to be sure that the patient fits within our criteria for
life expectancy. Then one of our nurses goes out to meet the
family and makes an assessment as to what is needed. The
kind of referrals we feel best about are those from families we
have already worked with. Now they know other people who
are in the same situation. That makes us feel good because it
says that we are doing something worthwhile, and people
recognize it.

The person is then enrolled as a patient of our hospice,
and we contract with the County Health Department for the
nursing services; that is, we obtain the financial support of

nurses for the terminally ill persons. We have another social worker besides myself. He functions as a social worker, while I function as the coordinator of the program. We have lots of volunteers for this program, and we train them ourselves. We go into a family and do whatever the family tells us it needs. That might be counseling; it might be nursing; it might be some very concrete services like getting them supplies or equipment or making sure that they have transportation. One of the nurses carries a beeper all the time, and one of us is always on back-up to the nurse. We have sat up all night in the hospital with a dying patient. We get out to the homes and are there when patients have died. We go to the funerals. We give the families every support we can give them, emotional, physical, spiritual.

You say some die in the hospital. I thought the hospice patient is at home, not at the hospital.

That's right. Hospice is health care outside the hospital. We support the family as much as possible, to keep the patient at home. Occasionally there is a medical emergency and the patient will have to come back into the hospital. That's happened with a few of our patients. Sometimes they've been here just overnight, or one day, and they die. But essentially, they've been at home for most of their illness. Our focus is not that the patient is dying, but on the fact that this patient is still living and is a very viable part of his family. That's why we put the emphasis on family. We try to give the family every support so that the patient can still retain his or her role in that particular family situation. We have to remember that many of the terminally ill are not always bedridden. One of our patients did fine for a while and went to work every day. We could support her in that decision. Another patient was still going camping up to a month before he died. We encouraged him, even to the point of a nurse saying, "If you want, I'll come to the campsite." We give them that kind of support because we want them to know that they are living and that they have much to live for. Even when they are about to die they are still a member of the family.

What is the economic level of your hospice patients?

It varies greatly. Some are very poor; some are very wealthy. If a family cannot afford a service, and they want it, they get it anyway. The criteria are short life expectancy, residence in the area, the fact that they want to be on our program, and that their doctor agrees to remain their physician. Ability to pay is not a criterion for admission. Surprisingly we have had a seventy percent reimbursement, which no one expected. It comes from the insurance companies, Blue Cross, Medicare, Medicaid.

We have more old people than young, and more females than males. Last year we had four children on our program, and we have two right now. So, we take patients of any age and with any medical diagnosis. Most of them have some form of cancer, but we've also had cardiac patients. Most of them have had some kind of hospital experience; and they are the people who don't want to die in the hospital among strangers, and hooked up to machines. I'm not belittling the quality of care given in the hospital. When you come to die it's a lot more comfortable to have somebody there whom you know and love, to take care of you.

Do people resist the thought of dying?

In terms of the hospice situation, my own experience has been that patients handle the fact of their death, in general, better than their family members do. They seem able to deal with it more honestly. The families have a tendency to hide it from them, to protect them, and the patient gets caught in the same game. One man said, "If she doesn't want me to know that I'm dying, then I won't talk about it either." We are very honest with our patients, and every member of the team takes that as a moral and spiritual duty. We treat them with a good deal of respect. As the chaplains always say, we start where they are and discuss things as they feel able. Some of them are very open and say, "Look, I know I'm dying and I think this program would help my family." And they insist on being in it because of their families. This is very interesting because sometimes family members will say they don't want us to be involved because "he doesn't know he's dying." Maybe it's really the family member who can't cope. It's very sad when someone you love is dying.

Less than one-third are bedridden much before the end, and less than that are in severe pain. We encourage them to keep up whatever normal activities they can. One of the goals of hospice is to keep the patient as pain-free as possible. Our medical director serves as an expert consultant on pain control. We work with the doctors in terms of regulating the medication, and allowing the patient to regulate his own medication so that he can be both alert and comfortable. At this point there is no need to fear addiction, and we want our patients to participate in the decision-making.

Do you get good cooperation from the medical doctors?

We have to educate doctors probably more than we educate anybody else. For one thing, this is still a fairly new concept, especially among the older physicians. The doctors in the oncology treatment center responded right away by making referrals. Now we're getting them from other physicians too, but we had to kind of prove ourselves and show them what we are about. We had the advantage that the daughter of one of our patients was a nurse for one particular group of doctors, and they learned how much we did for her father. She just talked about it so much that we now get a number of referrals from that group. Also, the fact that we are on call twenty-four hours a day gives the doctors some relief. Sometimes people call a doctor just for reassurance, and not for a medical problem. Instead, we are fielding those calls. If we phone the doctor he knows that it is for a legitimate reason.

How do you deal with a family that's reluctant to accept the fact of approaching death?

An example is a very lovely lady upstairs who will be going home soon. She is forty-five years old, is divorced and knows she is dying. Her two daughters living at home with her are seventeen and nineteen. The older one is handling it pretty well, but the seventeen year old isn't. Essentially, they are the ones who will have to take care of her at home. You see, mothers are not supposed to get sick and die; they're supposed to come with a warranty; they should not wear out and break down. So, here is an example of that situation being reversed. The kids are finding it very difficult to deal with the fact that their mother is dying. The roles are going to have to be turned around. They are going to become the caretakers, and she is going to become the dependent party. This lady and her daughters are already enrolled in hospice, and we'll be seeing a great deal of them from now on. This happens to be a fairly religious family, and this is the kind of situation in which our chaplain gives invaluable help.

What is meant by a bereavement program?

It's another term for a kind of organized grief counseling. When we accept the patient we are accepting the patient's family. We work with both, together, while the sick person is still living, and when the patient dies we still have the family. We have good evidence that family members who cooperated in the hospice program suffer much less grief than those who do not participate. Their mourning and sense of loss have been alleviated by the fact that both they and their dying relative were being emotionally and spiritually conditioned for the inevitable event of death.

The hospice staff stays in contact with the bereaved family as long as it seems beneficial, but the hospice volunteers actually organize them in two bereavement support groups, one for the bereaved spouses, the other for younger people. These groups meet informally once a month. They are able to work out their problems as a group effort, and they sometimes accept people who had not been in hospice while the family member was still alive but who also need grief counseling. These are very active groups; we put teenagers in touch with teenagers. Right now, we are planning a picnic for all these people to get the families interacting on a friendly informal basis with each other. They get to share names, phone numbers and addresses, and help each other out. They may feel more comfortable and draw strength from each other this way. We stay very active with these families for about two years after the death; and by this time most of them drop out, as their feeling of loss has greatly subsided.

XVII

Hospital with a Mission

*Reverend Eugene, Presbyterian min-
ister, is head chaplain at a multi-unit
Presbyterian hospital center*

Has your hospital center always had a chaplain's department?

Yes, from the very beginning, about seventy-five years
ago, when a Presbyterian pastor had the vision of helping the
tubercular patients in this area. Our tradition of pastoral concerns continues from that one man's vision. The primary purpose of our being here, and the main reason for the health
care we offer, is simply to reach out to human beings in their
time of need. From the very beginning we have had a chaplaincy program, and it is founded on a sense of Christian mission, compassion and charity, which I'm sure you have in
your Catholic hospitals too.

Now, there have been many changes over the years, and
we can no longer claim to be a specific enterprise of the Presbyterian Church. It began originally as a church-related hospital for which the funds were solicited mainly from many
local congregations around the country. The chief executive
for the first three decades was a Presbyterian minister. According to the corporation by-laws at the present time four
members of the board of directors must be clergy persons.
The center still submits an annual report to the synod but
does not get either funding or administrative direction from

the church. From an organizational and managerial point of view, I think we now have to say that we are non-denominational; but from the perspective of our pastoral care ministry, I prefer to think that we are interdenominational.

We have modernized our language and our methods, and we have become ecumenical, but we have not watered down our theological beliefs or our Christian mission. The last annual meeting of the Presbyterian Church synod restated the fact that the center continues as an expression of the Presbyterian Church's sense of mission. We have reached out to incorporate a number of smaller hospitals and clinics, and we are reminded that "the extension of the system to rural areas is an extension of the Church's call to mission." What I am saying is that this is not just another secular hospital that simply competes for customers with proprietary hospitals that exist as a business to make profit.

What is the clergy personnel of your chaplaincy department?

I am the paid full-time chaplain here, and we have another paid Presbyterian minister who works at our affiliate hospital in the mornings and comes here in the afternoon. Actually, this second position is also budgeted for full-time, and we'll fill it when the new administrator is in office. I'm an approved CPE supervisor and had a year's clinical training in the teaching hospital of a university medical school, and another year of pastoral internship at a large state hospital. Then I did a half-year refresher and updating course at our local Catholic hospital.

The supervision of trainees tends to take more time than I like, but the students are a genuine help in ministering to patients. I usually have eight or ten seminarians who get their lectures and academic work each morning at the seminary, and then come in five afternoons a week to minister to the sick. We have a rabbi who regularly visits Jewish patients. The Baptist minister you met volunteers two or three days a week for general calling on patients. One special kind of person is our Jesuit lay brother who had full training in clinical pastoral education and finds his primary mission here at the hospital. He is not on the hospital payroll, nor is the local parish priest who was appointed by the Catholic bishop and gets his salary from the diocese.

Father Tom is different from the other ministers around here. It is the understanding of the local parish pastors that whenever they have parishioners here in the hospital he is responsible for their spiritual welfare as long as they are here. So this frees up the local parish priests from needing to come in and spend a lot of time in the hospital checking on their sick people. Thus the Catholic patients receive regular spiritual pastoral care, and that's pretty well organized. Other patients indicate their religious preference on their admit card, and if they are Protestant of any particular denomination, or none, I or one of my helpers will visit that patient within twenty-four hours and ask, "Does your pastor or minister know that you are here?" If the person says, "Yes, my pastor was here this morning," we don't feel any compulsion to follow up.

Sometimes a pastor who goes on vacation, or expects to be out of town, asks me to pay special attention to his people while he's gone. He may ask me to inform him of a sudden change, or of a particularly severe prognosis, and I'll do that. In such cases we act as a liaison between the patient and the pastor, but only temporarily. My philosophy is completely that the local pastor, priest or rabbi is in the best position to minister to the spiritual needs of his people. He knows their background, where they're coming from and what follow-up is helpful. I don't see my role as one of competing with the local pastor, or repeating what he can do. Sickness is a temporary happening; people get well enough to go home; and our spiritual care of them is also temporary.

You said you took a refresher course in pastoral care over at Saint Francis Hospital. Do you continue contact with them?

Oh yes, I have very cordial relations with Sister Mary Louise who runs the chaplaincy department and is also a veteran CPE supervisor. We share essentially the same medical staff, so that any physician may well have patients in both hospitals. What may seem to be an oddity is that St. Francis closed down its obstetrics and maternity departments several years ago. Most babies born in this city now are born here. I understand this had once caused considerable distress among Catholic parents who wanted their infants born in a Catholic hospital. I think there is probably still some moral concern among the parents and priests because it is known that Presbyterian does tubal ligations when necessary, and also therapeutic abortions.

Meanwhile, St. Francis developed certain special programs in which they excel, like a strong oncology service with radiation therapy. They have the only acute rehabilitation center in the whole state. It is a focus on the care of neurological cases, the kind of disabilities that require long-term rehabilitation. Their department of home health care reaches out to many needy sick people who are confined to their homes. The most notable program to which we can give some pastoral care cooperation is their growing hospice program, which is also the only one in the state.

Do you have many lay volunteers to visit your patients?

Aside from the clergy there are people from the community who have a religious, or Christian, calling to attend to sick people. A minister's wife is here regularly two afternoons a week to help out on the children's ward. And another woman is a regular volunteer, a retired nurse who visits our skilled nursing facility one day a week and feels she has a calling to minister to elderly people there. We used to call that the "extended care" ward because they do not need acute care but are in a kind of transition to the nursing home. Some of the ministers in the area have what they call "health committees" of lay people in their church who minister to the needs of sick members in their homes, but also visit them when they are patients in the hospital. Of course, I myself don't have a church appointment outside the hospital, but on Sundays I try to be available to speak in churches of all denominations to acquaint them with the work of our chaplaincy and to give general encouragement for the health care of their members. I do quite a bit out in the community. I'm on the board of a jail chaplaincy ministry of the Baptist Bible College, and on two different counseling services outside the hospital that are church organized and church operated.

We have what we call Clergy Day twice a year at the hospital, and we send invitations to every pastor, priest and rabbi in the city and some even in the suburbs and outlying areas. This is a popular event because we will have members of our medical staff and our nursing staff speak to them on subjects that are relevant and helpful for the clergy in their visitation of sick church members. This is good also in another direction, in that it introduces the medical people to the fact that the clergy are professional people trained to deal with the sick, both at the hospital and in their homes. I am convinced that most hospital physicians hardly ever see their patients in the home setting.

What is your pastoral role in the network of smaller, so-called "satellite" hospitals out in the small towns?

You know that this is called a hospital center, and not just a hospital, because it is like the "flagship" in a whole fleet of other, and smaller, affiliates. I think the Seventh Day Adventists have a system of Good Samaritan hospitals; certainly some of the Catholic orders, like the Sisters of Mercy and the Sisters of Providence, conduct a whole network of hospitals. There are a lot of material advantages, economy of scale, or whatever. There's exchange of managerial know-how, and of the talent of surgical and medical experts. We can take referrals from the hospitals that don't have the large modern equipment that is so expensive. Now, I have a parallel notion—and it is still only a dream—that chaplaincy competence may also be shared throughout the system. We can expand our pastoral care training to provide refresher courses and experiences for the men and women in the smaller places. They would absorb the ideals and the healing mission that we foster at the center. Anyway, I think the multi-hospital system under one central management is the wave of the future.

We try to encourage the communities in which the hospitals are located to organize a corps of volunteer chaplains because there is no money to pay full-time people. I try not to be cynical, but it seems so often that the religious needs of people are supposed to be met only free of cost. At any rate, the administrator of the smaller hospital contacts the local ministerial alliance and invites them to the hospital to hear an address from me. It isn't as though they have to start from scratch or that the clergy have been neglecting their members who are in the hospital. Most of them do not have a tradition of lay visitors to the sick, and this requires some instruction about the functions of hospital visitation. We tell them our own experience as a basis for organizing and maintaining a volunteer chaplaincy program. Now, in the hospitals that have done this, the program has been well received by the administration and staff, by the patients and by the community. The clergy find this a very good means of involving their people in their Christian witness. I have been able to make only two of these trips a month, but, considering the limited time I have to put into it, I think this type of program has gone over very well.

Are you expected to act as chaplain to staff and other employees?

That is not in the job description, and the normal expectation is that we are here primarily at the service of the sick and ailing, and that the other people—doctors, nurses, orderlies, and all the workers—have church ties outside the hospital. It's a fact also that we have an excellent counseling department for the benefit of the patients and their families, but they too are sometimes called in to counsel employees. After saying all that, I must still admit that there are people working in this hospital who prefer to come to the clergyman, the chaplain, when they have some kind of personal problem.

Usually, these personal problems are job-related, like the person who has had a run-in with a supervisor and made a complaint of unfair treatment. Even though we have a grievance committee, and a counseling service, some people still prefer to come to me. There are some exceptional days when I have spent six out of eight hours with staff people in trouble. I try to listen very carefully, patiently and confidentially. Of course, the sick people come first in our attention, but in an indirect way we are helping them too because if we have satisfied employees we are likely also to have better patient care.

A large amount of my counseling with staff and employees is marital, and it seems that some people would rather not talk with their own clergyman about their marriage problems. And this too influences the way they do their job and relate to other people in the hospital. The role of the hospital chaplain is different from that of the marriage counselor, but I guess a clergyman is expected to help people in whatever trouble they are in. It is not easy to console the woman whose husband beats her and the children, has another woman on the side, and threatens to abandon the family. Even more difficult is the highly trained medical professional nurse or doctor who usually comes for spiritual guidance when their human relations entanglement is beyond repair.

I don't want you to get the impression that we have a bunch of emotional cripples working for the hospital. The fact is that the overwhelming majority of them are healthy, loving, caring people who are willing to cooperate with pastoral care. I came up with what I call an enabling model. We spend a great deal of time with these employees, especially nursing service and in-service programs where they learn to appreciate the whole personality of the patients, their spiritual and emotional needs. We try to enable them, as it were, to give them the confidence they may not have had in school or in other hospitals, so that they are competent in reaching the inner needs of patients. Some of them become exemplary Christian ministers to the sick without claiming to come under that umbrella.

Does the medical staff cooperate well with you?

Oh yes, I think that nurses and physicians know what to expect in regard to chaplain's work in a church-related hospital like this. If they had no regard for spiritual values they would be uncomfortable here, and probably wouldn't sign on in the first place. We get a good number of referrals from physicians. It's not unusual now for a doctor to write an order on the chart asking for the chaplain to see this patient. For a while I was making notes and comments on the nurses' chart, but the physician who was head of the medical records committee called me one day and said, "I think we need to develop an insert for the chart so that when I look at it I'll immediately see your notation you've made about my patient." So we devised a special page with a red border on it, so that the minute the doctor opens the chart he catches whatever I or the other chaplains have put there. I haven't heard of that in other hospitals, but I have passed that information on to friends of mine around the country.

Another thing I'm excited about is that many physicians with a patient who is malignant or terminal will come by my office and say, "I need to go up and talk with a patient's family. Would you go with me?" So we'll go up together. He'll answer the medical questions and give them necessary information and advice, and then tell the family, "The chaplain is here to be with you for a while and help you in any way he can." Then he excuses himself and leaves. So we get routine referrals from the doctors, and sometimes a personal and cooperative visit like this one. I think many doctors are embarrassed and uneasy when they have to give bad medical news to patients and their families. They have to do it, but they leave the tearful after-effects to the chaplain.

We get most of our referrals from the nursing staff who seem to know almost intuitively when the patient can benefit from the chaplain's visit. Now, if a physician specifically says "I don't want a chaplain seeing my patient," we can't go in to see that patient. But a nurse does not have to ask permission from the doctor to refer a patient to me. The only time I've been asked not to visit a patient, it was a person with a psychiatric problem, and the psychiatrist had said, "You can't talk to anybody except me." Of course, the nurse understands that completely, and so do I, but some of the ministers resent it.

One of the physicians said that not all ministers are welcome.

Let me tell you about the trouble I had with some of the Fundamentalist preachers the first couple of years I was here. I call them primitive "Bible-thumpers" who take every page of scripture literally. Most of these preachers are independents and have their own church. They may call themselves Baptist or Methodist, or even Catholic—they go by almost any label—but they are not affiliated with any of the large mainline churches. They often see the hospital as an opportunity for proselytizing members and as an opportunity for preaching and high pressure evangelism. They were the kind who tell the patients, "If you believed in Jesus, you would not be sick."

You can imagine what the administration and the medical people thought of that kind of religion. Groups of them were going door to door, visiting, preaching, shouting, healing, singing hymns. So one of my first responsibilities when I got here was to put a stop to it. Of course, I became the devil himself. When they couldn't get into the hospital they came as a group on Sunday afternoons to sing and pray and preach real loud just outside the entrance. After a lot of warnings we had to call the police to eject them. That made headlines for me in the next day's paper.

As a hospital with a religious mission do you provide health care for poor people?

I know for a fact that the hospital gives a substantial amount of free care, or charity, and it takes different forms. For instance, a typical case is somebody in an auto accident and the ambulance brings them to our emergency room. They have acute trauma and are treated. Many times these people have no funds and no insurance, and no way of paying their hospital costs. I have been made aware of the large amount of money that the hospital simply writes off. I've known people who have had extremely complicated surgery and were not able to meet the financial obligation. Nevertheless, the surgery was done, and the surgeons were willing to forego compensation for it. Now, I don't want to make any generalizations to cover all doctors in that regard.

There is another point to remember. The county hospital, which is affiliated with the medical school of the state university, is something like your Charity Hospital in New Orleans. It is tax-supported and funded out of state revenues, and has more of that image of serving people who are not going to be able to pay that facility. In other words, that's where indigent patients are expected to go, and that's where the ambulance brings them, more than to the other hospitals in the city. All I can say—and I pray for this—is that the poor are taken care of, both medically and spiritually.

XVIII

Born-Again Psychiatry

Doctor Maureen is professor of psychiatric nursing in the college of nursing at a large urban Catholic
university

How does psychiatric nursing bring God into the healing process?

I think that every health care professional can use technical skills and knowledge for the greater glory of God, which
is reflected in your love and concern for God's troubled children. What I mean is that you start from the premise that
every occupation that anybody has is a kind of religious calling directed to the benefit of mankind. I know that there are
nurses and there are psychiatrists who would say this has
nothing to do with curing sick people, and they go about their
work with no reference to this humane philosophy, and
probably would not understand your question. I try to explain this to the junior level nursing students I teach in psychiatry at the university, and I try to practice it fifteen hours
a week as a clinical specialist at St. Joseph's Hospital.

Let me answer your question with a recent experience.
The nurse called me to intervene with a lady whom she
termed a "nervous wreck." She was the wife of a thirty-four
year old black man, who had surgery for glioma, one of the
worst malignant brain tumors anyone can suffer. The nurse
said if I didn't come in and do something with her they were

going to forbid her to stay with her husband. He was a truck driver who had had a pain in his head for several weeks that caused him to vomit and to stagger, but he went to work every day. The wife took him to seven different hospitals trying to get someone to say that her husband's headache wasn't just a headache. Anyway, he was post-operative but still in serious condition.

She was beside herself but was willing to pray while she cried. They were Catholics who hadn't been to church in ten years, but they had both returned to the sacraments. Anyway, I put my hand gently on the incision on his head and I just prayed for a healing of that tumor, but, more importantly, I prayed that the pain of that headache be removed. Healing could better happen if the pain was gone. He came out of his coma and said, "My pain went away right then." I believe it was the pain that incapacitated him to be awake and to be comforting his wife and to be talking with me. So I think that Jesus wants to really heal and relieve pain that makes people irritable, crabby, angry at God, denying of help.

Can you separate the psychiatric approach from the spiritual?

No, I can't in real life situations. My theoretical framework I draw mostly from Viktor Frankl, the Viennese psychiatrist who had been incarcerated in a Nazi concentration camp. He is probably the only classical theorist in psychiatry who talks about those neuroses that come from moral conflict or spiritual conflict. Frankl sees an existential vacuum in people who are depressed or obsessive or alcoholic or hypertensive or ulcerative or whatever, as much out of the spiritual realm as out of the physical or the emotional realm.

Freud says that man's will is toward pleasure. Adler, Sullivan and the neo-Freudians say that man's will is toward power. Frankl says that man's will is toward meaning. In his explanation of logotherapy he says that we only fulfill ourselves when we find meaning in our existence and experiences. He gives examples to demonstrate that we can find meaning in suffering. He has an answer too on the combination of religion and psychiatry when he says that "people who nowadays call on a psychiatrist would have seen a pastor, priest or rabbi in former days."

The theodicy problem is always with us, and I think there has to be an explanation for suffering, but it is just not always visible to us. Where I am struggling with suffering is when some theologians say that pain and suffering is always evil, but that our attitudes to it can make it redemptive. I guess I am struggling with some of the more positive aspects of suffering because I have tuned in very much to the whole movement for healing. I do lay hands on people. I do pray for healing. I have seen healing happen.

You relieve pain and you pray for healing. Do you also see a value in suffering?

Suffering is part of the human condition, but I don't think its universality is evidence that it is a good thing. Yet we Christians firmly believe that our ultimate salvation with God in eternity was gained for us through the passion and death of Jesus. Even during the agony in the garden we realize that what he went through was endurable, at least by him. I am trying to recognize two levels of suffering: one that can be borne and is redemptive. In other words, I think that suffering that is powerful or that is really redemptive is the pain that can be borne. Secondly, I'm suggesting that if the pain is so bad that it can't be tolerated, or that the person wants to commit suicide, then it is not redemptive.

In a book called *He and I* Jesus talks to Gabriel Bossier, a French woman, and says that at one point along the way of the cross his face was so disfigured by tears and pain that even his disciples didn't recognize him. That may mean that we don't always see God, or any divine meaning, in our suffering. It may mean also that Jesus gives some people the power to accept suffering that is redemptive for others. There is the legend of St. Lawrence enduring the pains of fire. In the beginning of his autobiography Ignatius Loyola talks about the butchery—if that is his word—when his leg had to be reset, but he never uttered a complaint. He was a brave man, embracing pain that would leave most of us screaming in the aisle. I personally would want morphine and to be put out.

Isn't it true that medication in the form of narcotics has removed most of the physical pain in modern medical practice?

Yes, in the hands of a humane and knowledgeable, and empathetic, medical staff, the physical pain can be reduced enormously, but I've seen cases of mutual recrimination between nurses and physicians about the use of sedatives. There is still a popular phobia about uncontrollable drug addiction resulting from the use of narcotics, and some doctors and nurses seem to have a callous attitude to pain. Some patients will react equally to a placebo as they will to seventy-five milligrams of Demerol. I am called to deal with some patients who are such a nuisance about pain that they are given placebos. Then they complain that the injections are not working, and they are labeled neurotics. If they're Hispanics they're called manipulators; if they are Jewish they are always complaining; if they are black they are looking for a high.

All across the board I think we are missing the fact that pain, post-operative especially, needs to be treated with a narcotic. You can't get up and walk and support an incision if that pain is ripping you apart. The nurse can come in and rearrange a pillow and talk to the patient, and that's supposed to make him feel better, but the patient needs a hypo. The nurse says the doctor forbids it.

The surgeons tell me they write the order for pain medication as PRN, which means apply "as necessary." They say the nurses all seem to interpret that as "when they ask for it." The overcautious nurse then makes people in pain have to beg or ask again and again. What I'm saying is that the medical staff has to use all their technical knowledge to allow healing and to help God to do the healing.

Ultimately, then, does it come down to divine intervention?

Yes and no. You're putting it much too simply. There is a great deal that we human beings can do in cooperation with

God. For instance, the patients I visit are not always emotionally disturbed or mentally mixed up people. I come into the hospital room and offer my presence as a sign of caring and healing. The second thing I can offer are my psychiatric skills in taking a look at what might have been some of the wounds and the anger and the bitterness that may have led to that particular physical disease. I can help them explore what was happening in their lives at the onset of this illness, whether it is tuberculosis, sore throat, pneumonia, angina, whatever. What were some of the angers and resentments and hurts of their lives that may have been part of, or a causative agent of, this disease itself?

I think we are going to come more and more to know that man's attitude, inability to express anger, to deal with feelings, has a great deal to do with all illnesses. You can't escape that if you believe that man is one whole human being. In other words, if you think that man is just a psychological being, or just a physical being, or just a spiritual being, then what I am saying will make no sense to you.

In general, America seems to deny the holistic principle. Our whole western society does. We have spent billions of dollars erecting and maintaining clinics and hospitals that butcher and chop out and medicate the human body, and ingest poisons and toxins, absolutely denying that man is spiritually sick and emotionally sick, and that these sicknesses are being acted out by the physical body.

Aren't you really doing the chaplain's work?

Not if you accept the principle of health care as holistic, without the conventional separation of the spiritual and the physical. I don't mean to be derogatory. I guess I see everybody struggling for a role. I see a lot of people hurting who are uncomfortable with the role that is assigned to them, so it is an easy thing to slide out of it. I think that some of the chaplains, who are trained, try to deal with the emotional and psychological too. Sometimes they do it very well and sometimes very poorly. I think a number of chaplains are uncomfortable with the spiritual, so they try to play the emotional role.

You must know Paul Pruyser's study of the *Minister as Diagnostician*, where he insists that clergymen are failing to bring their theological and spiritual treasures into the field of health care and are substituting psychological counseling for religious ministry. I also see that happening. I think that many of the clergy are themselves kind of wounded and are uncomfortable in praying with people and in laying hands on people, so that they've gotten into the psychological. I consider it a mistake to switch from one to the other if you are unable to combine the two.

Let me say that I see some healthy changes in the development of pastoral care teams, for which seminarians, sisters and priests are now being well trained. The medical staff is now more open to include the chaplain's team in the care of patients well before they die. In the old days they said, "Quick, get the chaplain, or the pastor, because they're about to expire." Or, if they had already died, you got the priest to comfort the family. I think also that now the nurses and the doctors are more ready to call the pastoral team to give people support who are in for a two-week stay, and who walk out healthy.

Some time ago I heard a priest speaking at a luncheon, who said that historically nurses have been healers of the body, and chaplains have been heralds of the word. He said the time has come when nurses need also to be heralds in addition to healers, and chaplains need to be healers as well as heralds. We all need to expand our role that much more, to bring the oneness that says "Jesus is healer." The two words must be said together. We as healers must really be willing to say, "I bring Jesus with me, in my touch, in my voice, and how I change a dressing, whatever I do."

Are the nurses in your hospital attuned to your highly spiritual interpretation of health care?

As a registered nurse I am probably more attuned to them than they are to me, and I'm also the one who helps them out when they can't handle difficult patients. Furthermore, I am there with them as a clinical specialist in psychiatric nursing. Sometimes there are patients who are acutely suffering so that the staff nurses feel they can't reach or touch them. They say that if I would come down and speak with them, and pray with them, and see the family, maybe I could help in ways that the staff nurse feels she cannot help. So I have good contact with the nurses when they need me and when they can observe the significance I place on the spiritual aspect of patient care.

Let me give you an example of an eighty-nine year old lady the nurses asked me to see one day last week. The staff said she was hysterical and dramatic, and over-reacting, because in fact her congestive heart failure wasn't really that bad. She was depressing everybody because she said she wasn't going to leave the hospital alive. The nurses thought she was being suicidal or was being manipulative in order to get a lot of extra attention. I told her that the nurses really love her and that they were worried about her talk of not leaving the hospital alive. She began to cry and I asked her, "Are you ready to die?" She said, "Yes, I pray for it every day."

In the next fifteen minutes I came to discover that she had been grieving because last month, within one week, she lost a fifty year old niece who was like a daughter to her, and a fifty-two year old godchild. She was grieving because they were too young to die, and here she is eighty-nine, praying for death, but God keeps her alive. We began to talk a little bit about the mystery of Jesus' suffering, and what a mystery it is that we do surgery on young children, pray for their healing, but they die, while here someone like herself is ready to die but stays alive. She said she's been a widow for forty years, and prays three rosaries every day. She prays for the doctors and the nurses, and for all the sick people in the hospital.

I said to her, "Have you any idea how many souls those three rosaries a day have saved, or how many people you don't even know are really helped by your prayers? So maybe you are the only one in this time and place that the Lord can trust to stay alive and pray those rosaries so faithfully every day. Maybe your niece and your godchild had even more suffering than you know." She said, "How did you know that?" Well, I didn't know that the niece had had a severe mental breakdown and had been struggling in pain for years, and that the godchild had suffered terribly from arthritis.

I think I did two things for her. The first was that I got her to focus off the negative notion about not leaving the hospital alive and instead affirm her good relationship with God. The second was that I reassured the nurses to lay off, and to realize that this was a normal old woman getting ready to meet God and grieving the loss of two people who were very dear to her.

You give the impression that you are pretty critical of nurses.

Maybe I feel that I'm allowed to be that way because I'm talking about my own people. I'm a registered nurse; I've been through the experience of every department in the hospital, and I have a lifelong interest in the progress of the nursing profession. But I certainly don't want to leave you with just critical and negative impressions. The registered nurse today is more and more frequently earning also a BSN, a bachelor of science degree in nursing, and gets a deeper knowledge of health care and the whole medical field to complement the essential training in the hospital itself.

Another contemporary advantage that we have introduced here is the concept of primary nursing. This supplants the collective approach of team nursing that was very popular after World War II, where a nurse leader would direct a group of assistants to care for fifteen to twenty patients. All of our units in this hospital are now on primary nursing, which means that the nurse personally does everything for three or four patients. This is more costly than the team approach but it also provides a better quality of nursing. In other words, this puts the registered nurse back at the bedside taking care of the sick person from the time he comes in to the time he goes home.

Let me leave you with an idea I picked up from a couple doctors at the Harvard Medical School. In one of their monthly *Health Letters* they said the doctor himself, or the nurse, can be an effective placebo in place of writing a prescription for medicine or drugs. "The placebo effect is one of the best examples of a mind-body interaction, in which thoughts and beliefs are translated into body changes." The good "bedside manner" of a doctor or a nurse can put the patient's mind at rest, cut down the perception of pain, and make healing and recovery more rapid. This is an important aspect of psychiatric nursing, and it can be a real contribution by the chaplain.

It's a regular pastoral pattern at St. Joseph's Hospital that in the morning before a surgery the doctor talks with the patient about to be operated on and then has the chaplain also give assurance and confidence to the person. Now we have some pretty good evidence that the anesthetist needs only about half as much pain-killing analgesic, and that the patient heals more quickly and can be discharged earlier from the hospital. I don't like to call this the prevalence of mind over matter, but it is an understanding that giving drugs is not the only proper way to practice medicine, and that the technical skills of doctors and nurses can well be supplemented by the spiritual contribution to health care.

XIX

God in a Medical School

Father Joseph is head chaplain, campus minister and professor in the medical school of a large state university

How did you come to have several jobs at once?

The assignment started off as campus ministry to the university medical school that has a teaching hospital connected with it. As I translated that into action I felt that it was not meant to be just another Newman Center having Mass and the sacraments for Catholics, but an influence on all the students who are going to be physicians. So I started a program for all of them, not just for the Catholic population. I titled it "Ministry to Medicine" and worked it up with an Episcopal minister. We do voluntary discussion programs at noontime on some current topic that comes up in the medical world which has ethical implications.

It's a fairly informal program in the sense that I've been around the place for about ten years, and I know the people I can ask to get into it. For instance, if the topic is something in neurosurgery I can get a brain surgeon to talk about it, or about any of the areas of medicine and surgery. Then the students get into the discussion to pick up the ethical aspects of the problem. Over the years we have covered a lot of areas of medical ethics, and in the process I've also kept my eyes and ears open to infiltrate the mammon of iniquity. In the meantime, I got a part-time staff assignment as adjunct professor of community medicine.

Under that aegis I am called the coordinator of human values in medicine, and I run a program that is basically ethics. It's an odd fact that both professors and students get itchy when you say "ethics," so you use a more general term like generic medicine. You don't want to get them too excited or worried. If you say ethics and morality they think about the priest preaching, and they turn you off. This program now is part of their regular curriculum, eighteen clock hours in the first year and nine clock hours in the second year. It isn't a great deal of exposure, but the nine two-hour sessions in the first year take a look at the problem areas in their clinical materials.

This is to prepare them eventually for their humane treatment of the patient. The human values component is precisely there in the relationship between the health care deliverer and the sick person. Perhaps this isn't spirituality in the strict sense of prayer and religion, but the thrust of the program is really: "How do you treat your fellow human beings?"

Where does God come into this program?

He doesn't come in, that is, in the general program because it's for everybody and you can't peddle it as God. But the Ministry in Medicine program definitely comes across as being religiously oriented. There's no problem there identifying yourself as being Catholic, or my associate as Episcopal, and we say clearly that "the Church teaches this or that." Anyway, we treat it as a development of what we call their value system. We confront them with the need for consistency in their value principles, and obviously there will come times when they want to know objectively, "What does the church say about this?" That's the type of voluntary program the Episcopal minister and I have going. Luncheon is the most common time for doing that.

As part of the Ministry in Medicine I run a specifically

Catholic program that has Mass three times a week at the chapel of the medical school. Occasionally we'll run a prayer service for some of the non-Catholics there. We get a fairly decent attendance, all things considered. It is up and down. The medical school is, of course, a tight ship, and you have to run your program at a time when they can come. For example, they have one hour off for lunch, so I have to guarantee them that if they come to Mass they will be out in a half hour, then have their lunch and get back to class. So we have Mass at 12:05 and get them out at 12:30. It gives me a chance to get some of the Gospel to the Catholics anyway. Some of the staff people come too, secretaries and occasionally a professor, especially on holy days.

What I'm saying about the lectures and the discussions, and about the Mass and the preaching, deals only indirectly with the spirituality of the patients. But there's another way in which we can do this. First of all, as I said, we deal with the general treatment of the patient, but we also try to indicate the value of an interdisciplinary approach to the care of the patient. I mean that the nurse, the physician, the social worker, the nutritionist, but the chaplain specifically, must be there. The so-called interdisciplinary rounds assures us that all aspects of the patient's condition are considered.

Are you involved in actual pastoral care?

I have to say I am not a CPE trained person, and when I was in the seminary we never had this kind of field work. This started out to be a chaplaincy to the medical students to prepare them to have a humane concern for patients. I soon realized that if I am going to talk reality and not just abstractions I must have direct contact with actual patients. So I go twice a week to the oncology section of the hospital in which they do experimental oncology. These are people who have been written off in the sense that medical science can do nothing more about their cancer. I see all of them, whether they be Catholics or not. If Catholic I always take care of the specifically Catholic aspect, their duty with the sacraments, and so forth. If they're not Catholics, I talk with them and let them ventilate, see what their spiritual posture happens to be. If there is some relationship to prayer in their life I try to help them out on that. They may want to hear the scripture, and I read the passages they want.

Visiting with these patients and caring for them spiritually gives me a sensitivity to the human reality of suffering. I'm not just talking about patients as they are written up in the medical books. I go there on Friday, and when I come back on Monday I find that two or three of them are gone, because that's a section where people don't last long. So I visit those patients and sometimes they die in my presence. This morning I had a reconciliation ceremony with a patient who received Communion. Another patient asked for the sacrament of anointing as well as Holy Communion. A couple of the non-Catholic patients just wanted to talk about their children. The people I deal with on that section are a very select group, and most of them pretty much know that they are at the end of the line. In this process too I get to know some of the staff, and it was out of these contacts that we developed the interdisciplinary kind of approach. Not all of the doctors cooperate with us, but those who do say that they are happy about the way it works. This is the kind of exposure for which we want to enlist more and more of the medical students.

Out of my experience I have definite notions about hospital chaplaincy. Patients expect certain kind of talk from the chaplain that they don't expect from a doctor or a nurse, or a social worker. You come in as chaplain, no matter what label you wear, and that says to them a man of religion, a man of God. From the standpoint of the church that is the value of the chaplain. He is prophetic. You don't see this, for instance, among the nuns doing chaplaincy work who have this penchant for not wearing the identifying religious habit. I think they've got more problems in this direction because to the patient they are not immediately recognizable. It's just another woman who comes in. She has a sign on her that says "pastoral care" but they're not sure what that really means. So she tells the patient, "Now, I'm a chaplain," and if it's a Catholic he'd say, "Oh, so you're a nun." Now I don't want to run down the nuns, but I'd say a priest has that initial advantage because they accept him as a priest. They think of him as a minister, or as a priest, or in any case as a man of God, and therefore the concepts of prayer and spirituality are quite natural.

Do you think that most doctors are religious believers?

Well, probably not, but I would make some distinctions, I guess. You know Rahner talks about the anonymous Christians who may not have their theology straight. A lot of people—and maybe doctors especially—have a kind of magical concept that they put on God. You know, you wear a medal and you get a miracle, that kind of thing. Maybe they get that notion from the way they see some of us peddle religion, and when they see that they can't buy it. I think that most doctors, who are theologically pretty ignorant, believe in some sort of power beyond themselves. That also is a kind of labeling, and maybe in the long run it's a purer notion of religion than the one that some of us may seem to demonstrate.

I also believe that the training the doctors go through, and the very physicalism of medicine, has a tendency to make them into materialist and physical beings. So that God is out of their categories, everything must have its biological significance, especially because they are trained in the so-called scientific method. Once you specify what constitutes proof, then God is kind of out of the picture, because it is a sense-proof that they are after. So they say that they can't prove God in that way.

But some of the younger physicians, and some of the medical students, now are beginning at least to listen. They don't read much non-medical literature, but they pick up news stories about healings. Several years ago we had big discussions about Kübler-Ross, who thought she could prove the future life. Perhaps she goes to the opposite extreme to prove that these people have gone to God and talked to him, and have come back. We had a lot more sensible discussion among the students about Paul Tournier who is a medical man and a true religious believer. His book on *The Healing of Persons* made a real impact on some of the medical people around here as they began to realize that there is a lot more to health care and healing than expert medicine.

How does the medical student change during his four years here?

I've been here long enough to watch quite a few classes go from freshman year to senior year, and there is a kind of pattern that fits most of them. They end up with a kind of "pragmatic idealism." You remember that big research study of medical students, *Boys in White,* that came out of Kansas in the early 1960's. It didn't study religious or spiritual attitudes we're talking about, but it was quite typical. When the new student comes in the first year of medicine, he does have idealism about pain and about alleviating suffering. But then everybody he sees suffers, and he has to take care of all of them. He begins to look at the statistical things that he can do. What chance does this procedure have over this other one? He's figuring on the best medical thing to do.

I am sure that the first patient he takes care of, and who dies, just crushes him. After that, as the second one gets closer to death, he wants to share the experience. This is why I feel that an interdisciplinary approach in medicine is really a requirement. That's the only way you can die a little bit with each patient if you have somebody suffering with you. After all, we are dealing with frailty, and we have to deal with the fact that we are terminal beings. To put it in a more pragmatic way: How many times can you die? As a chaplain, or even as a medical person, nurse, nutritionist, physician, pharmacologist, you have to be part of the suffering. I have to die a little bit with every dying person. Generally, we are reluctant to see any patient die, but when all of them on the staff agree, "We know this is all we can do for him," you're not going to put a code on him when he goes into an arrest, because we know that nothing can be done for him.

What do you mean by a "code"?

Well, the hospital has a procedure that goes over the public address system when you hear the words, "Code Blue in Room so-and-so." To the staff that means that you drop everything and rush to this room to resuscitate the patient. It becomes in some respects almost a travesty. Here's a person trying to die and they're pumping on his chest and putting needles into him and electric shocks. Now, when a person has been beat up by a truck and is brought into the emergency room, you put every effort into pulling him through. That's one thing; but when you see a person you know has been progressively dying and is prepared to die as much as any human can be prepared to die, or at least for whom you have no prognosis that you can give him any help, that's another thing.

Often there is really no point in trying to prolong life. When the nurse comes in and finds there has been a heart arrest, she shouldn't have to call the code. She could just give him something to comfort him. If he's in pain give him some pain medication. If he's gasping for air give him oxygen. But don't try going to resuscitate him. The problem is that no individual is going to call this decision. It is much easier when it is shared by the interdisciplinary group.

Let me give you one example. We had a sixty-three year old woman with a severe tumor. She had gone through surgery to reduce this tumor, and by now they couldn't do anything more for her. They had her on chemotherapy which sometimes succeeds but often fails; and even this was not showing any results. Then they invented something called hyperalimentation which is a super-duper intravenous diet. Most intravenous infusion is just to maintain a person, but this is a kind of super-feeding. People actually gain weight on it, which is almost considered miraculous. So they wanted to use it on this lady because they thought at first to try some further treatment on her. She had been maintained for almost four months in this hospital and no hope was being offered except to try another treatment. Each time they did it, something else was being deteriorated in her body.

One of the nurses who was very upset about it came to me and said, "What good are we doing with this patient?" I said that the first thing we've got to realize is that this patient is conscious and is able to make a decision for herself. Then we called the doctor in and asked him, "What does she know about her case? Does she know that none of these treatments now have any validity, that she is just being kept alive to do her dying longer?" We thought he should tell her the facts, which he did. After that she said, "Okay, I see that what you're doing is nothing more than keep me here as a patient and keep my husband always on edge thinking that something is going to happen. Well, just put me on ordinary pain control, and that's all, and I'm ready to fade away." Within a week after that she was dead. So, there wasn't any use to code her or do anything extraordinary to keep her alive.

Can't they let such people go home to die?

That's another angle I'm working on as a long-range education plan in both the medical and the pastoral field. The patient gets good pastoral care while in the hospital, but when he comes home he is neglected. They take him off the parish prayer list, and parishioners who visited him in the hospital don't visit him at home. In most cases I think that's when he needs more help because he doesn't have the supports he had in the hospital with nurse and chaplain, and doctor, and everybody else. Maybe the family is not helping him and maybe the family also needs a lot of support. One of the reasons is that the parish priest really doesn't know what to do for the person who has come out of the hospital. He's not trained for that.

Because of the work I do, I am a member of the local Catholic Hospital Association of this diocese. I'm also on the board of the Diocesan Department of Christian Service, in which we have a Committee for Human Services. The educational aspect is the training of lay volunteers in every parish to visit their sick in the hospital. The nine Catholic hospitals in the diocese have their own lay auxiliaries working together with the parish volunteers, and they are trying now to have an organized group of lay visitors for each of the other large hospitals. But I don't think that any of them have extended it so these people could visit at home, when a person comes back from the hospital.

The kind of program I'm talking about, from an academic standpoint, goes further than this and needs a lot more training. I think the great need is in the homes of people in the first place, for ex-patients or convalescents, but also now when we are sure that terminal cases are a lot better off dying at home. That is easily said, but wherever you have a hospice situation you have to train the members of the family how to take care of the sick person. That family and those relatives need moral and practical support that can come from professional home care people, but there is always a place for trained volunteers to give assistance.

Does the diocese have a program to train and provide more hospital chaplains?

The answer is a bit complicated because it goes beyond the willingness and the ability of the diocese to answer this need. In the first place, every major seminarian—and they are not as numerous as they used to be—has to do a certain amount of field work in hospital chaplaincy. Quite a few women religious want to take the full program of clinical pastoral education, and we have some young parish priests who want to do the same. So, there is not a shortage of potential chaplains or associate chaplains, but the most serious drawback is the unwillingness of many hospitals to pay for a full staff of professionally trained people in pastoral care.

Historically, the main focus of the hospital was to care for poor people who couldn't afford physicians, and the care was more spiritual than medical. In the last hundred years or so medicine became more scientific and more effective in healing people, and well paid, while the clergy came as volunteers to visit the sick. The point I want to make is that the diocese and some Protestant churches foot the bill in supplying chaplains to hospitals. My feeling is that the public sector respects what it pays for. When they get the chaplain free, they say, "That's fine; it's wonderful; of course, we want him here but we don't know what he does because we don't pay him anyway."

That's why I want to get this academic responsibility behind us so that we can say that we have trained people ready for full-time and well-paid chaplaincies. At every opportunity I state in public and in private that an authentic hospital must have a chaplain staff that meets professional standards like anybody else. The salary should be a professional salary. Obviously, we want spiritually trained people but we also want them to have the qualifications for the job. If he's paid they'll listen to him. He can make statements at staff meetings, organize and talk about holistic medicine, discuss the spiritual needs of patients and the morality and ethics of hospital medicine.

Meanwhile, the Catholic diocese can pay for a limited number of trained chaplains for non-Catholic hospitals and can assign part-time chaplains from the nearby parishes, while the Catholic hospitals pay for their own pastoral care departments.

XX

God Is a Coping Mechanism

Doctor Marilyn heads the department of child psychiatry in the teaching hospital of a large university

Do most psychiatrists take religion seriously?

Most of them take it seriously because they often have patients who seem to be harmed by religion and others who seem to be helped by their belief in God. You know that there are committees on religion and medicine all over the country. The impetus for these groups seldom comes from clergymen, and the medical doctors who originate such meetings and conferences with the clergy are almost always psychiatrists. Internists and surgeons are not particularly interested in such groups because the discussion always centers around mental health, the professional domain of psychiatry.

I don't think this proves that psychiatrists are religious persons. It is my impression that many of them are non-believers, or at least they don't go to church regularly. Many scientists are non-believers, but many of them, especially in the helping professions, have respect for people who are believers and church-goers. In other words, most psychiatrists think that religion is sometimes useful in dealing with patients. They don't see the irony in making use of an instrument which they don't believe really exists. I'm not saying this very well, but while they may not believe in the existence of God they realize that this belief is often helpful and useful in the lives of their patients.

Of course, I am convinced that man has the need to believe in a higher power, whatever that is, something greater than himself. I think it was Voltaire who said that "if there were no God man would have had to invent him"—or her, as the feminists insist. And of course, Freud thought that God is a human invention. Perhaps the psychiatrists who have been tremendously influenced by Freud just accept the notion that human beings who are distressed and in need simply reach out for a powerful being when they need help. It seems to me that in every age and every civilization people have always sought God, and history shows that they have found him.

Are you active in the church?

I guess you could say that. I was a choir member in my younger years; then I taught Sunday school in the parish all during college and even while I was in medical school. I have been a member of the vestry in my parish church. I am now on the bishop's council, the executive board of the Episcopal diocese. The highest honor and duty I had in the church was to be one of the four lay delegates to our general convention. These are external activities that seemed quite logical for a member of the church to do, but I want to add that beneath these externals I have a strong faith in God. I was brought up to believe in and make use of prayer and the sacraments. So, my Christian faith is very personal and not just churchy.

It's easy to say that religion is good for my patients. I can tell you it's also good for me. Medical doctors, physicians and surgeons, see a great deal of suffering and have to cope with it if they are going to get on with the job. Maybe they are sometimes sustained by their faith in God. A psychiatrist needs even more support. I was an internist, a family physician, for almost ten years before I got into psychiatry, and I can tell you that patients who are mentally ill put a lot more pressure on you than somebody with appendicitis or a broken leg. It takes much more time and effort—and with less assurance of success—when you're dealing with mental patients.

I am not sure how other psychiatrists react to this different and heavier pressure. People talk about the incidence of suicide among psychiatrists, and I wonder whether this is the attempt to cope with stress and pressure on one's own. I find that God is the best coping mechanism—if you'll excuse the expression—and that's part of the reason I can answer your question affirmatively. I am active as a religious person. Besides that, I think it is quite reasonable for everyone to have a relationship with the Creator.

Religion is good for you, but what does it bring to the healing process in your patients?

People with a strong religious faith are usually better equipped to deal with frustrations and disappointments and suffering. My understanding of religion is cheerful and upbeat. So, an optimistic, hopeful patient who is able to handle his or her feelings is a lot more likely to get well than a person who is gloomy and pessimistic. You remember William James' discussion of the "sick soul" who always looked on the dark side of life. This is a very difficult type of patient and is a lot less able to fight illness. So the same sickness—or what looks like the same sickness—will have very different manifestations in these two kinds of people. Insofar as religion is experienced in a hopeful way the patient can be measurably and more quickly improved in health.

The fact is that illness causes regression in all of us. When we are seriously sick we all start to feel helpless; we are fearful of losing the love of people who are important to us. In a sense, we become dependent and almost childlike; we are afraid of being abandoned. So, if religion gives us the faith and confidence to persevere in spite of our fears and our anxieties, it is tremendously beneficial for a person who is trying to get well. You don't heal well or fast when you are full of worries and fears. As someone said, fear can change discomfort into real pain. In other words, you get worse instead of better.

Another thing we ought to realize is that illness usually tends to cause either grief or depression in people. In the consistently "sick soul" it is likely to cause depression, but in the "healthy soul" it will just cause grief. Those terms are not up-to-date in modern psychiatry, but you know what I mean. Grief is a normal human response to loss, and illness constitutes a loss for people. Obviously, it's a loss of health, and often a loss of freedom, to be with one's loved ones, to pursue one's interests, to work at one's job. It interferes in your life's routine. Sometimes there is a loss of self-esteem and self-worth. When your body isn't working right you may begin to question whether anything about you is OK. You see, a lot of our ego is "body-ego," so the normal response to such loss is a feeling of grief.

Now grief is different from depression. Sometimes the sick person suffers depression at the loss of health. This happens when a person's coping capacities can't manage the feelings that loss stirs up—the anger, the sadness, the anxiety, and the guilt. When this happens we suffer pathological depression rather than just a normal state of grief. The difference between grief and depression is that there is a serious lowering of self-esteem in depression. With grief you can still have good feelings about yourself, but with depression you feel worthless and helpless.

Do your child patients get depressed?

Sickness occurs in people at any age of life, and it always includes a loss of self-determination and feelings of loneliness and helplessness. Yes, little children can become both fearful and depressed. I had a six year old boy patient with a fatal illness. He had a lot of trouble settling down at night after his mother left the hospital to look after her other children. He couldn't get to sleep, and he explained to me that he was afraid to say his prayers. What frightened him was the part that said "if I should die before I wake." That really hit too close to home because he had sensed that he was very, very ill. So he needed to talk with somebody about that. I got him to change the words of his prayer so that he said, "Hold me now on starry night; wake me in the morning bright."

This child needed to enjoy what life he had rather than get anxious and worried about the fact that he was going to die. Youngsters respond to sickness differently, according to their developmental stage and to the kind of experiences they've had in the family. There is no set pattern, but children who have a good relationship with their parents do tend to emulate their parents and take on their parents' values. So a child from a religious home would be more likely to value religion if there is a good, loving relationship with the parents. If it is a bad relationship, children might want to be the opposite of the parents. They might want to turn away from religion because they're angry with their parents or feel that their parents have not met their needs well.

What children think and how they conceptualize things and see the world depends a lot on their developmental stage, and we are hearing a lot from James Fowler about that. I find that children are very interested in religion. They have a lot of curiosity about everything, about God and religion, about life and even about death. They tend to turn to adults to help them understand things that are confusing to them. How can God be everywhere? Where did God come from? So it is quite logical for children to ask questions about the nature of God and to try to understand how their parents feel about these matters.

Children are particularly inclined to ask such questions when they are under stress, such as when they are ill, just as grownups sometimes question whether the sickness they're experiencing has any meaning for them and they turn to religion looking for an answer. Perhaps we adults don't realize that children can have some very deep thoughts and that they too wonder about religion as a source of meaning in their lives. Here again, we see that they may obtain satisfactory answers to their questions, and we must not expect them to have sophisticated theological understanding. Indeed, most American adults seem to have a little more than a Sunday-school knowledge of religion.

I assume that you deal with the parents of your patients.

Oh, indeed. Child psychiatrists always work with the parents as well as with the children. We don't always talk much about religion and church, but most parents have a respectful, if vague, notion that it's good for the children to have some religion. This shows up strongly when the child is seriously ill. Having children seems to awaken religious feelings in parents, at least while the youngsters are little. There seem to be very few atheists among young parents, but there are some people who misunderstand, or misuse, religion.

Now and then I'll encounter someone who uses religion very badly to justify certain practices that may be damaging to the child. For instance, they'll quote "Spare the rod and spoil the child," and they probably never heard a quotation like "Provoke not your child to wrath." They know the Bible, and they always find the right passage that supports their conviction. If they're beating up their kids all the time they want you to think that they're doing it out of love and concern for the child. They call it loving discipline. They don't want to look at the fact that they are setting the child an example of violence, teaching the child to be violent, or that they're conditioning the child to feel very depressed or very worthless.

This doesn't happen very often, but I have dealt with a few parents who are using religion inappropriately to justify doing something damaging to their child. They are reluctant to admit that the child's behavioral disorder may be a direct consequence of their own behavior, that they are making the child very anxious, or that their child may even be suicidal because they are being beaten up too much. I want to stress the statistic that the great majority of battered children do not come out of religious families. The extreme cases that come more and more to public attention are the children of parents who are themselves much in need of psychiatric attention.

I do a lot of public psychiatry and do lots of consultation with agencies that deal with neglected, damaged and battered children. Child psychiatrists tend to spread themselves

as thinly as they can because we are in short supply. I'm involved in the community in various ways. I go to one school
for retarded youngsters, and I go to a couple of residential
treatment centers for anti-social boys. Public psychiatry
means helping people with psychiatric services for which
they cannot pay. At the mental health center I can see a certain number of children, but I also consult with the staff and
help with the in-service training for the staff. Most of the
graduate students in psychiatric social work get some training at such locations.

*Do you ever have patients for whom religion itself is a psychiatric
problem?*

Religion is such an important part of life that it is not sur-
prising that when people become psychotic there are religious delusions manifested in their psychopathology.
Sometimes these cases are quite harmless—except to the patient—but are difficult to deal with: the woman who claims
she is Joan of Arc, the man who is convinced that he is St.
Francis of Assisi. You can't blame religion for that any more
than you can blame the humanities for the disturbed scholar
who claims to be William Shakespeare. Interestingly enough,
such delusions are not common among children even though
many tend to have vivid imaginations.

I don't want to find fault with biblical literalists, but I
wonder about people who are willing to test their faith by
handling snakes or drinking poison. Some of the more drastic
sayings of Jesus affect some people, like the statement that
rather than sin "it is better to go into eternal life maimed." I
know of one psychotic patient who quoted the Bible and at-
tempted to pluck out his own eyes. That sort of thing can be
very tragic, but that's a misunderstanding of religion. Certainly it's a tragic mental condition, and the person who is
"off" on religion is usually also off on everything else. It
would be a mistake to argue that religion is somehow the
cause for this mental disorder.

Of course there are some far-out fundamentalists who
don't hesitate to say that sin is the cause of sickness. "If you

give yourself to Jesus, you wouldn't be sick." The best thing to do with these fanatics is to keep them out of hospitals and clinics. The Christian Scientists are more subdued in their behavior but they seem to be equally doctrinaire. Sometimes they call me when they are really hurting. They get scared, you know, but they always wait to call me in the middle of the night, and they always consider that they have somehow failed in their religious beliefs if they had to have a physician help them.

The extremists among the faith healers do no good to either medicine or religion. The modern charismatics or pentecostals are something different. A lot of the churches have healing ministries, including yours and mine. Morton Kelsey has been as sympathetic as anyone among their critics and takes a very balanced view of faith healing. You know that the charismatics report organic cures only occasionally; their wider success seems to be with psychological or mental problems. They talk about "healing of the memories" and the importance of improved human relations. As a Christian I am ready to believe in the power of the Holy Spirit to heal the sick.

As a psychiatrist, do you deal with functional illness separate from organic illness?

Well, you can't really separate them quite as cleanly as that, because every physical illness has some emotional sequels or consequences. You might say also there's a kind of causal pathway that leads in both directions. Emotional stress leads to physical tensions, and these tensions may then lead to physical illness. Some persons who have emotional difficulties may not be in touch with them, may not be able to own their feelings and deal with them, and they use body language to show that they have functional illness as well as physical illness.

This doesn't mean that you make yourself sick, although some popular writers suggest that. It means that you are not able to keep yourself well if you are overwhelmed by your feelings. That's when you resort to body language. If our stomachs go into a knot so that we have pain in our abdomen and maybe too much acid secreted in our stomachs, we can have functional illness. It is very similar to physical illness and can even become physical illness. Ulcers start out as emotional problems, and they can wind up as very dangerous and serious physical problems. So those psychomatic disorders that are functional illnesses, or disturbances in physiology originally, are very important too.

Let me get back to the healing properties of religion. Aside from God's power to perform miracles—about which I have no doubt—the practical utility of religion is that it helps us to put up with adversity, including sickness. I think that religion can be helpful in healing people, but it is not necessarily the direct means for bringing about a cure. The more important and lasting function is that it prepares us to accept life's vicissitudes and to do the best we can to deal with them. Everybody has problems in living and could use a little psychiatric help occasionally. The ability to cope with emotional problems is often the means for avoiding both functional and physical illness, and that ability is supported by religion as well as by psychiatry.

You obviously recognize a close relation between religion and medicine.

It is only in the last few centuries that a clear distinction has been made between religion and healing. You know that Ivan Illich makes a strong case for this historical fact and tends to put medicine in second place. The priests ceased to be the healers, and medicine gradually became a separate profession. Psychiatrists are now attempting to deal in a scientific way with the same kind of mental anguish and emotional distress with which the professional clergy were always concerned. Certainly religion and medicine have a lot of similar aims and methods. They both develop helping professionals who are guided by systems of belief and theory. It seems to me that they are parallel in many ways and really should work side-by-side to help sick people.

Religion has demonstrated its usefulness over and over

as a means to find meaning in life, and can do a lot that psychiatry can't do. In psychiatry we deal more with conflict, and we try to help people resolve these inner conflicts, whereas the religious professional can really help people deal with existential anxiety. We have to limit ourselves to the level of neurotic anxiety, while the clergyman goes far beyond this and into more important areas of life's meaning, our place in the universe, the large question of human destiny. Psychiatry does not pretend to handle considerations of such magnitude.

Many of our ministers and priests among the hospital chaplains like to quote Carl Jung, who said that his patients got sick because they had severed their religious roots. He believed that if they want to become really healed they have to renew their contacts with religion. On the other hand, there is an ongoing argument about the substitution of psychology for theology in the pastoral care of the sick. I don't like the tendency to make a complete separation between the two. I think it is good for the chaplains to make use of psychological insights in ministering to the sick, but I think it is also good that psychiatrists use religious insights in relieving their patients of emotional and mental problems.

Index

261.8321
F445

Lincoln Christian College

74675